THE GIANT AT THE FORD
and Other Legends of the Saints

BY THE SAME AUTHOR

Land of Heroes: A Retelling of The Kalevala
A Margaret K. McElderry Book

The Giant at the Ford
and Other Legends of the Saints

URSULA SYNGE

Drawings by Shirley Felts

A Margaret K. McElderry Book
Atheneum   1980   *New York*

Nihil obstat ANTON COWAN, *Censor*

Imprimatur DAVID NORRIS, VIC. GEN.

Westminster, 11th July 1979

The Nihil obstat *and* Imprimatur *are a declaration that a book or pamphlet is considered to be free from doctrinal or moral error. It is not implied that those who have granted the* Nihil obstat *and* Imprimatur *agree with the contents, opinions or statements expressed.*

LIBRARY OF CONGRESS CATALOGING IN PUBLICATION DATA

Synge, Ursula. date.
The giant at the ford.

"A Margaret K. McElderry book."
SUMMARY: Recounts the lives of both well-known and lesser-known saints, many of them women, including St. Christopher, St. George, St. William Firmatus, and, St. Odilia.
1. Christian saints—Legends. [1. Saints]
I. Title.
BX4658.S96   270 [B] [920]   79-23026
ISBN 0-689-50168-4

CRC BX 4658 S96 1980
Copyright © 1978 by Ursula Synge
All rights reserved
Manufactured by Fairfield Graphics, Fairfield, Pennsylvania
First American Edition

CONTENTS

Introduction 7

The Giant at the Ford, St. Christopher 9

Zita and the Rich Man's Cloak 22

St. Jerome, the Lion and the Donkey 37

Odilia and Aldaric 48

St. Moling and the Fox 64

The Farm-Labourer Who Wanted to See Jerusalem 71

St. George and the Dragon 86

St. Mochae and the Bird from Heaven 98

Queen Sunniva 106

The Flying Walking-Stick 120

William Firmatus and the Savage Boar 128

St. Senan 137

Werburgh and the Troublesome Geese 150

St. Paul and St. Antony 160

St. Wulfric, the Boy and the Bread 175

Sources 183

INTRODUCTION

Saints are not ordinary people. They are men and women whose whole lives are so totally committed to God that the very air they breathe is not quite like the air we know but is permeated with the presence of divinity. He or she may be humble, untaught, unknown, or one of the mighty and powerful ones of the world—a queen, an emperor or a pope—but they have this in common, that for them God is the only reality and his service the only way of life. And this quality, wherever it shows itself, is recognized. People have loved the saints and tried to emulate their lives, or they have hated them and even killed them—but only very rarely, if at all, have they been indifferent.

The lives of the saints fill many volumes, rows and rows of books on library shelves. Many are historical and factual accounts of events witnessed by contemporaries—and many others are purely legendary. And, because saints attract stories to themselves in much the same way as kings and heroes do, there are marvellous and perhaps unlikely tales attached to people who really lived.

My choice of stories was far from easy. The same tale is often told of more than one saint—St. Paul, it seems, was not the only desert recluse to have been buried in a grave dug for him by two lions, and the story of St. Werburgh's geese is also told of St. Milburga who founded Much Wenlock Priory in Shropshire, England, and who, like Werburgh, was a granddaughter of King Penda of Mercia. I found, too, that others beside St. Zita were said to have given their masters' cloaks to beggars at church doors.

Why then did I choose to write of this saint rather than that one? To answer that is no easier than my choice. Perhaps these clamoured for a hearing more loudly than did the others; perhaps I loved them for their humility or their humour or for something in them that can speak to us all—or perhaps it just seemed to me that their stories were good ones, worth handing on.

And if you were to ask me if these stories are true, I could only reply that if they are not, then they should be, for goodness is true and so is humility and so is love, and if goodness and truth and humility and love cannot work wonders, then there may be no wonder in the world at all but only cold facts and concrete. I could not bear to believe that.

Ursula Synge

The Giant at the Ford
St. Christopher

Men said Offero was a Canaanite, and he may well have been, for there were indeed giants in the land of Canaan in old times. And this man was certainly as huge and brawny and fierce as any giant.

He appeared at the King's house one day and said that he was looking for the greatest and most powerful man in the world, that he might serve him, and that he would serve no one less. The King's steward looked him up and down and thought to himself that this fellow would make a fine champion; the very sight of him would make the strongest adversary quake.

'You have come to the right place,' he said. 'On God's earth there is none greater than my master.'

'I will see for myself,' said Offero, and he strode into the King's great hall, while the King's picked guard stood aside to let him pass.

The King sat on a golden chair and his feet were on a golden footstool. He wore a crown and his robes were woven with gold thread, but he was a small man—a puppet beside Offero—and he trembled beneath his weight of gold.

Offero was no speech-maker. He went right up to the King and asked him bluntly, 'Are you the most powerful ruler in the world?'

The King cast a glance from right to left, but his guards were looking the other way; they did not wish to tangle with a giant before they knew which way the wind blew.

At least I can die with dignity, thought the King, and he answered firmly, 'I am.'

'Then I will serve you,' said Offero, and he went down on his knees before the King and put his two calloused hands between the King's bejewelled ones. Now he had all he wanted.

It was an easy service, he found, with little enough to occupy him. When the King rode out, Offero walked at his bridle; when the King feasted, Offero stood behind his chair. Apart from that there was nothing for a champion to do beyond eating his fill and playing at dice with the men-at-arms. He issued a challenge from time to time and offered to fight any who would stand against him—but few responded. And even those few unaccountably melted away before the wrestling-ground had been prepared. None the less, Offero was satisfied. To serve the mightiest ruler in the world was no mean thing.

There were entertainers at the King's house—a girl who walked on her hands, and a man who ate fire, and a dwarf who danced with a muzzled bear. There were singers too. Sometimes they sang of ancient battles and voyages, of a woman whose magic turned men into pigs, of a widow-wife who each day wove a web and each night destroyed it. And one night a minstrel came wandering out of nowhere and sang of a man who was tempted by Satan. Offero thought it a fine tale and Satan a clever fellow, so he looked at the King to see what he might think. The King leaned back in his golden chair and picked his teeth with a little golden spike, and smiled. But whenever the name of Satan was mentioned, he made a solemn face and, with his right hand, crossed himself.

'Why do you do that, master?' asked Offero.

'For fear of Satan,' said the King. 'This sign that I make above my breast will protect me from the Evil One.'

'If there is someone that you fear, you are not the greatest and most powerful man in the world,' said Offero, scowling. 'You have deceived me, master, and I will call you master no more.'

He took his club on one shoulder and a sack of provisions on the other, and left the King's house without another word.

For seven days he walked and encountered no one. Then on the evening of the eighth day, he met a man who waited at the turning of the path—and this man greeted him by name.

Offero grunted.

'I will walk with you,' said the man.

'Please yourself,' said Offero.

'I think you may do me a service,' said the man.

'Not I,' said Offero. 'I am the mightiest champion in the world and will serve only the greatest and most powerful ruler.'

'Perhaps you have found him,' said the man.

Offero spat. 'I thought I had,' he said. 'But they lied to me. Even the King of this world is afraid of Satan. Therefore Satan is mightier than he, and when I find him I will serve him, but I will serve no other.'

'I am Satan,' said the man, and there was something in his face that caused Offero to believe him.

So they went on together. And in every village and in every town there were men who gave all they had to

Satan—even their souls. Moreover, even when Offero entered a place alone, he was given the best of everything, for men said to each other, 'He has the air of one who walks with the Devil. Do not offend him.'

It was a grand life, he thought, better than standing behind a king's chair to watch jugglers, better than walking beside a king's horse. Satan was not only a generous master but excellent company—he could show Offero the whole world at once; he could whisk him through the air and make the stars sing for him.

'I would rather serve you than any king,' said Offero.

But one day they came to a place where stood a wayside cross—and Offero noticed how his master made a wide detour to avoid its shadow.

And another day they came to a stone building with a cross above its door and Satan turned back a long way to find another road.

'What is that sign?' Offero asked him.

'I saw no sign,' said Satan, blustering.

'Aye, and you did,' said Offero. 'A sign like this and like this.' He made a cross in the air with two great sweeps of his arm. 'It seems to me you do not like this sign.'

Satan shuddered. 'It is because Jesus Christ died on such a cross as that,' he said. 'When I see it, I cannot help but tremble. He is my enemy and I am his—and it is foretold that he will overcome me in the end.'

'Then you lied to me when you said you were the greatest and most powerful,' said Offero, with bitterness. 'You are scarcely greater than the little King I served before I met you, and all my time with you has been waste and folly.'

'What does it matter?' asked Satan. 'You enjoy my

company. I have given you power and pleasure such as few men ever have; what is it to you if I will not pass a church?'

'It is everything,' said Offero, shouldering his club. 'I vowed to serve only the most powerful, and you are not he. It seems that this Jesus Christ, whether he be alive or dead, is more powerful than you are. Therefore I will go in search of him...'

So he went on alone. It was a long journey and a hard one. He performed feats of strength in the villages to earn his bread, and at night he slept in outhouses and barns or under the stars. More than once he missed Satan's companionship, and more than once he missed the easy living of the King's house—but he kept straight on.

Everywhere he asked the same question: 'Where may I find the greatest ruler in the world?' but the people shook their heads and could not answer.

'If we knew that,' they said, 'we would serve him ourselves and have servants of our own. But our masters have masters over them, it seems, and the overlord of all must be very far away. If indeed there be anyone who has no master...'

After many days and weeks of wandering, he came to a hermit's hut in a wild and lonely place where it seemed impossible for a man to stay alive at all.

Offero hammered on the door with his club.

'I fear I have lost my way,' he said to the old man who came out to him.

'That depends where you are going,' said the hermit. 'but in this world, all ways are much the same.'

'Yet this world is all we know,' said Offero. The hermit smiled.

'I am seeking the greatest ruler in the world,' said Offero.

'Then you have found him,' said the hermit.

Offero looked about him and saw only rocks and stunted trees, and he looked at the old man who was as frail and brittle as a dried straw, and as ragged as the poorest beggar.

'Here?' he asked. 'You?'

'Not I,' said the hermit. 'Yet I serve him.'

For a moment Offero's heart failed him, for it seemed that the greatest ruler in the world must use his servants very ill. But then he looked at the old man's gentle face and saw that his eyes were not those of a man who serves a hard master.

'I too will serve him,' said Offero. 'Tell me what I must do.'

'You must repent your sins,' said the hermit. And Offero grinned, then threw back his head and laughed until little stones came rolling down the hillside.

'Why, that's easy,' he said. 'I have had time enough for that in my travels. I have spent wakeful nights in which my sins loomed large in my mind and paraded themselves before me like soldiers before a king. They were sorry entertainment, I can tell you, and I am glad to be done with them...'

'You must fast and pray,' said the hermit.

'That is more difficult,' said Offero. 'If I fast, I shall lose my strength and that is all I have to bring to the Lord's service. No, my good friend, I may not fast.'

'Then pray,' said the hermit. But Offero still shook his head.

'I do not know about prayer, brother. I have never been a man to beg my master for favours, but have always held that if I work honestly at whatever I am told to do, then I will be paid for it honestly. So I served the King and so I served Satan—but I prayed to neither. Tell me how I may *work* for this Lord of ours.'

'I cannot say,' said the hermit, after much thought. 'Yet the Lord who guided your feet to my hut will surely enlighten me. We will sleep, good brother, and in the morning I will tell you what you must do.'

Offero would not sleep inside the hut for fear he should thresh about him in the night and bring it tumbling about their ears, so he lay in the shadow of a rock and listened to the sound of the river running nearby.

At first light, the hermit roused him and said, 'The Lord spoke to me from the swift stream. Follow the water for two days and you will come to a ferry—but the man who once rowed travellers across is dead, he was gathered to his fathers more than a moon since. Take his place, Offero, and when men ask you to name your fee, say to them that it is in the Lord's service that you take them across, and accept no payment.'

That sounded foolish to Offero. He said, 'But if I take no payment, how shall I live? I might as well fast first as last...'

'There is a hut and a field,' said the hermit. 'You have strong hands and a strong back. You will be obliged to no man.'

Offero followed the river for two days and, on the evening of the second day, he came to the ferry-place, where the road ran down to the water on one side and went away again on the other. The field was overgrown with weeds and the roof of the hut had fallen in but 'What has been built once can be built again,' said

Offero. That did not trouble him.

The condition of the ferry-boat was more serious. The rush of water in the springtime floods had driven it against a rock and smashed it. Dried out, it would make fine kindling wood, but nothing better could be said for it.

'Then I must carry the travellers on my back,' said Offero, and he cut a stout staff to bear his weight and hold him firm in the swirling water.

So he lived for many years, tending his field and carrying men to and fro across the river. To each he said, as the hermit had bidden him, 'The service is freely given for love of the Lord who is my master.' And some thought this a good joke, but others listened seriously and, themselves, set out to serve the same master in their different ways.

Then there came a night in the winter's dark when the rain poured down in torrents and the river rose to the height of its banks, roaring like a wild beast. Offero was glad to close the door of his shelter and light a fire for warmth—a small fire can be a great comfort on such a night.

He had scarcely settled himself when he heard a knock—a very small knock, low down on the door.

'A trick of the wind,' he told himself. 'No man would travel abroad in such weather, or knock so low.'

But it came again, and Offero knew that he would not be able to rest until he had answered it. He opened the door and looked out. The rain drove in his face, stinging his eyes and almost blinding him.

'Who's there?' demanded Offero, and the wind howled and mocked.

'Nothing,' said Offero to himself. 'No one.' And he closed the door. The fire looked more inviting than ever. A pot of broth hung on a chain above the flames, and the smell of it pricked his nostrils.

'No sensible man would be out of doors on such a night,' said Offero again. But once more the knock sounded and it could not be mistaken. Offero sighed deeply and went to the door a second time.

'Whoever you are, you had best come in,' he said, and stood aside. Then he saw that his untimely visitor was not a man but a child, and a poor, half-drowned scrap of a child at that.

'Why, you're blue with cold,' said Offero, and lifted the child in his arms to carry him near the fire. 'It's a sad thing to be lost at any time . . . but at night . . . and in such a storm. . .'

The child weighed no more than a feather.

'You'll be better with hot food inside you,' said Offero. He poured broth into a wooden bowl and the child drank, wiping his mouth with the back of his hand. Offero noticed that the hand was wounded, and the feet too, and thought of the thorny road the poor wight must have travelled.

'Sleep warm now,' he said. 'Tomorrow we'll find your kin.'

'I must cross tonight,' said the child.

'Not so,' said Offero. 'Tomorrow is soon enough. The river's in spate, and the road is as dark and rough on the other side as it is on this. The wind will have died by morning and, in the sun's light, you'll not be lost for long. . .'

'I must cross tonight,' said the child again.

'I doubt that even I could stand firm in this flood,'

said Offero, 'and a few hours can make little difference either way in a long journey. You are trembling and anxious now, but when you have slept you will feel better and see that I am right.'

The child went to Offero and laid his wounded hand on the man's knee.

'I must cross tonight,' he said. 'If you will not carry me, I must go alone.'

Offero's heart was against going, his reason was against it, his very limbs were against it.

'Look,' he said. 'See the good sense in what I say. We may both drown in the flood, and what use to us would our haste be then? If we do not drown, we may freeze, and die of an ague on the other side...'

But the child looked directly at him, and Offero took his cloak from its peg.

'You're one who knows what he wants,' he said, and grinned to keep the child's spirits high. Then he wrapped his cloak about the little, shivering creature, took his staff from its corner, and opened the door to the wind's blast.

'Climb on my back,' he said, stooping. 'And hold tight round my neck. Stay firm however I may stumble, and do not be afraid. I'll get you across somehow.'

And in his mind he said, 'Lord, I think you will need another ferryman soon, for even if we get safe across, I will not leave this child till I have seen him in good hands.'

Then he stepped into the water.

He had expected the cold, yet the shock of it made him gasp. He had expected the wind, yet the force of it almost threw him. The water reached his knees, then his waist, then his chest. He was in mid-stream, and battling with

the current, clinging to his staff and pausing a long time between each new step.

Fallen branches, carried downstream in the race, buffeted him. The river-bed shifted beneath his feet.

And the child, who had weighed no more than a feather, hung from his shoulders like a sack of iron, growing heavier as every minute passed. Offero had carried many fat countrymen in his time, and returned again for their produce, but he had never known such a weight as this.

'Half-way...' thought Offero. He felt as though his lungs were bursting. His hands ached with the cold, and he needed to use both now to hold his staff, for the water threatened to wrench it from him.

'We are half-way over,' he said, aloud. 'Trust me, lad. I was a strong wrestler once. I'll see you safe...' and then he kept his breath for the work.

It was the longest, most painful work he had known. He could not see the shore before him nor, when he looked back, could he see the shore behind. There was nothing in the whole world but the dark, raging water, the shouting wind, and the dragging weight of the child.

But the child's hands on his neck guided him, and the child's safety was all he cared about.

Offero's progress grew slower, his pauses longer, the child heavier. The night could hardly have grown darker nor the waters more treacherous, yet it seemed they had. He stopped thinking, even those thoughts that come into the mind unbidden.

One step—pause. Another step—pause. A deep, racking breath—pause. Stones shifted beneath Offero's feet.

He stumbled and steadied. Another step—pause.

No skilled wrestler had ever thrown him; he would not let himself be thrown by a mindless mass of water— nor by a wind, however powerful.

And at last the crossing was made. Offero leaned against the slimy, weed-hung bank and bade the child scramble to firm ground.

'I'm spent, lad,' he said. 'I'll stay here till I get my breath again—then we'll go on together.'

For the first time, the child obeyed. Then, kneeling on the bank, he caught Offero by the hair and dragged him up beside him, and Offero was too exhausted to think this an unlikely thing. He lay on the muddy ground and was glad to feel it along the length of his body—good, safe, reliable ground. He almost slept. Almost. But something still troubled him.

'You're a most uncommon weight, lad,' he said, sleep thick in his voice. 'I've not carried the like of you before.'

'Nor will you again,' said the child. 'For I carry the weight of the world's sin on my back. And this night you have carried it too.'

Offero looked at the shining child and at the wounded hands and feet, and felt such gladness in his heart that he could have danced.

'Why,' he said, 'you are the master I have served these many years. And I did not know you.'

'Yes,' said the child. 'I am called the Christ. And you have been called Offero—which means Bearer.'

'Why, so it does,' said Offero, sitting up and laughing. 'I had never thought of that.'

'From this time on you will be called Christopher,' said the child. 'Christ-bearer. Travellers will remember your name for as long as they remember mine.'

Zita and the Rich Man's Cloak

Goodness seems to run in some families—as blue eyes or a certain sort of nose or a manner of speaking runs in others—and it was so with Zita's family. Her uncle Graziano was a holy hermit, her elder sister became a Cistercian nun and Zita herself was a saint.

She was born in the village of Monte Sagrati in Italy and lived there until she was twelve years old. After that she had her own living to earn. Her mother had taught her all the skills she would need in life; she could cook and sew and clean and make polish with beeswax, she could bake bread and make medicine from herbs and she knew the difference between a common ague and an illness that was more serious.

'A good servant is worth more than treasure,' said her mother, and, with help from the priest, found her a place in the household of Pagano di Fatinelli, a prosperous silk-weaver in Lucca, about eight miles from Zita's village.

'It's a decent Christian family,' said the priest. 'If Pagano has a fault, apart from his quick temper, it is that he tends to spoil his servants. But that need not worry you. Zita is an honest girl and won't let herself be idle.'

He smiled indulgently at Zita. 'Your mother has brought you up well. See that you do her credit.'

It was all arranged. Zita's father gave her a pair of shoes as a parting-gift, which made her very proud as she had never owned such a thing in her life. None of the other girls she knew had shoes. Her mother, who had already given her much, now gave her a great deal of excellent advice, beginning, 'You are a lucky girl...' and ending '... always have a care for those less fortunate than yourself.' Her sister kissed her on both cheeks and said, 'I will pray for you, Zita.' And her uncle Graziano, the holy hermit, said, 'Do what is pleasing to God, child, and you will displease no one.'

Then Zita was ready to go, with her small bundle in one hand and her new shoes in the other.

'It would be a shame to dirty them so soon,' she said. 'But I will put them on when I reach the first houses. I promise I won't shame you with my country ways.'

'Country ways never shamed anyone,' said her mother. 'And that's something else you had better not forget.' And then she wept a little, for it is never a comfortable thing for a mother to see her children grow up and go away into the world, to live among strangers. But of course, Zita was not a child to fret over; she was twelve years old and very capable.

'Eight miles is not such a great distance,' Zita said. 'I may be able to visit you.'

It was something to think about but not to promise, because eight miles one way is also eight miles the other, and there might not be many whole days free.

At the house of Pagano di Fatinelli, she was welcomed by her new mistress and taken to the kitchen where she was given something to eat.

'What! before I have earned it?' she said, overcome by such kindness. Her mistress laughed, patted her shoulder and said, 'I am quite sure you will earn it child.'

Zita ate quickly. She wanted to begin work at once and she could see there was much to be done. The kitchen was a fine big room, nearly as big as the Church of Monte Sagrati, but it seemed sadly neglected—the fire needed mending but there was no wood set by the hearth, there was dust in the corners, flour spilled, pots waiting to be scoured, and surely that was a cobweb waving in the draught from the door.

The other servants seemed quite unconcerned. They said, 'Oh, let the work wait a while. It will all be the same tomorrow. Mistress doesn't notice so long as her linen's clean, and the master only rages if his dinner's late.'

Zita said, 'I think I would rather work if you will let me.'

'Shall we let her?' said the man.

'Might as well,' said the cook. 'If that's what she wants to do.'

Zita had to find the broom for herself, no one troubled to show her. She swept the floor and the hearth, brought wood from the yard and water from the well, scoured the pots with wood-ash till they shone, and was just about to scrub the table when the cook said, 'That's enough! It blethers me to have you fretting about like a great buzz-fly. Sit down now, do.'

The manservant came up from the cellar with a pot of ale he had drawn for himself.

'You'll soon learn our ways,' he said to Zita. 'And it's not such a bad place, you'll find.'

'I like to work,' said Zita, timidly. 'I was brought up to it, you see.'

'She *likes* it,' he said. 'Well, let her get on with it then. There'll be less for us to do.'

* * *

So Zita worked hard, and the house had never looked brighter. There were always fresh rushes on the floors, clean linen in the presses, wood stacked ready for burning. The pots and platters were burnished and the meals were always on time. And she was happy. She sang as she worked. She said her prayers every morning when she rose and every night when she went to bed; she wore her shoes to church on Sundays and thanked God for her good life. And four times a year she walked the eight miles to her parents' house, to let them know that all was well with her.

But she was not entirely easy with the other servants. They had been idle before and they were even more idle now, yet they were far from satisfied. Zita was too particular for them, and she had lost her timidity. When she saw the manservant selling good kitchen waste to a furtive fellow at the yard door, she spoke her mind. That waste should have fed the master's pigs, or been sold on the master's account, or given to the destitute of Lucca, who were dying from lack of food—it was most certainly not intended to enrich an idle servant who, in any case, had no need of money, being fed like a fighting-cock from his master's plenty.

'The devil save us all from this pious brat,' he complained to the cook. 'Let her do what she likes with her own, pray every night till her eyes drop out—and I wouldn't stir a finger to help her find them—but just let her not interfere with us.'

The cook told her, 'Eh, perhaps you mean well, but you're still a chit of a girl, and touched in the head besides. Get on with what you have to do and leave us be to manage our own lives. We did comfortably enough before you came.'

'We do very comfortably now,' said Zita. 'We have a good master and a kind mistress and, if the weavers were as idle as we are, we would none of us have a place. Why, if it weren't for them, we ourselves would be beggars at the church door.'

To be a beggar was a terrible thing—to need work and have none, or to be too frail or crippled to work. Pagano di Fatinelli and his wife were charitable people, they gave to the poor and grudged nothing. But the poor multiplied.

'I am grateful for what I have,' said Zita. 'Warmth and shelter and work. It would be showing a miserable spirit to God if I leave all the giving to the master.'

So every day she saved half her dinner to give to the beggars of the town, and some days she gave it all.

'It suits you to be thin,' said the manservant, one evening. 'I've never cared for a scraggy woman myself, but devil take me, you're different!' And he caught at her as she went past him, and tried to kiss her.

Zita was angry and frightened. She cried out to the cook to help her, but the cook laughed and said, ''Tis only fun. You and your uppity ways.'

It was certainly not fun to Zita. This man was forever talking about the Devil, swearing by the Devil, calling on the Devil to witness every word he said. Now he was like the Devil himself, with his red face and greasy mouth, and his horrible hairy hands.

'God help me,' whispered Zita, and she tore at the man's grinning face with her finger-nails, so that he cursed and let her go.

'She's a match for you,' said the cook, who was taking no one's part. 'Even if she is a praying zany.'

* * *

The next day the mistress noticed the scratches on the man's face and asked him what had happened.

'I will not lie to you, mistress,' he said. 'It was the wench from Monte Sagrati. Last night something caught fire in her head and she attacked me while I sat at supper. Get rid of her, mistress, before she does something worse.'

Pagano's wife was a gentle and tolerant woman, but she was also shrewd. She sent for Zita and asked for her side of the story.

Zita said, 'It is true I scratched the man's face,' and she would say nothing more though the mistress asked her again and again why she should have done such a thing. Then Pagano came and shouted that he would have no brawling among his servants, a man must have peace in his own house if nowhere else.

'And God knows I am a patient man,' he stormed.

'There! Now you have grieved your master,' said his wife. 'I do not know how you have the heart to do it, you vexatious girl.'

Zita hung her head and let the blame wash over her. If she told the whole truth the man would be dismissed and he was such a weak and foolish creature he would surely fall into an evil life.

'I do not know what we shall do with you,' the mistress said. 'You say you are truly sorry, and I believe you, but how can we know that it won't happen again?'

That was something Zita could not answer. If necessary she would defend herself again, but she could not say so.

'Will you send me away?' she asked. Perhaps it would be better so, though it should break her heart, and her mother's too. But better that than the alternative, a man's life broken and his soul lost.

'Oh, no,' said the mistress. 'We will not be so hard on you. What do you say, husband? We cannot send the child away for a first offence?'

'Let her go without her supper,' Pagano said. He could think of nothing worse, nothing more likely to promote a repentant spirit. 'And be warned, Zita, it must not happen again.'

What had begun ill ended well. The servants could not believe at first that the girl had taken the whole blame on herself, and they waited for the master's rage to reach the kitchen . . . but all was quiet.

'Why?' they asked. 'It's true you were making a great fuss about nothing, but you could have stood up for yourself before the master. Any one of us would have done so. . .'

'It would have been giving that man to the Devil entirely,' said Zita. 'No one has the right to do that to another.'

'She's a fool,' said the yard-man. 'She might have lost her place.'

'Well, she didn't,' the cook reminded him. But they all knew she had taken the risk.

After that their feelings changed towards her; they laughed at her less and respected her more. The cook admitted aloud that there was sometimes sense in what she did—it was better to go into the cold yard to fetch wood than to let the fire die out, it was easier to scour pots after use than to wait until they were needed again. . .

'And it is easier to make candles by daylight,' said the

man. 'She's too good for the likes of us.' It suited him to scoff a little, because he was ashamed. But he did not worry her again.

'That girl is growing too thin,' said Pagano's wife. 'Her eyes are almost bigger than her face.'

She questioned the other servants and learned that Zita was giving her food away. That year there were more beggars in Lucca than ever before, poor country people driven by famine into the town.

Pagano himself went into the kitchen to make the girl see reason.

'It is such nonsense,' he said. 'If you feed a beggar today, he will be hungry again tomorrow. It never ends, and if you do not eat, you will soon be as useless as they. What then?'

'I have work,' said Zita. 'I may eat whenever I feel the need. But if I do not share what I have with those who are truly hungry, then all my prayers for their comfort are worthless.'

Pagano threw open a great cupboard and shouted, 'See! Here are beans! A great store of beans! Take a few from these next time your pity for the poor prompts you to starve yourself.'

Zita was so grateful she could have kissed his feet. Now she need turn no one away. When the beggars thanked her, she said, 'It is from my master's bounty and by the grace of God.'

And the store of beans dwindled daily.

'You'll be in trouble,' said the cook. 'Master did not mean that you should use them all.'

And at last there came a day when Pagano di Fatinelli announced that he had found a buyer for his store of beans. They must be weighed and put into sacks without delay.

'Now you'll have to answer for it,' said the cook. 'When I looked this morning there was scarce more than would fill a skillet.'

'He will understand,' said Zita, but privately she was not sure that he would, and the cook was very sure that he would not.

'You know his rages,' said the cook. 'You've gone too far this time, my girl, and he'll surely put you out.'

They could hear him coming—his quick impatient step and the jangle of his keys. Zita trembled and cast an anxious prayer to heaven—Oh, God, you know the poor must be fed, let him not be too angry.

Pagano came in, smiling and rubbing his hands. He had bargained for a good price, one that was fair to both buyer and seller. He was satisfied.

He opened the door of the cupboard, and Zita closed her eyes. She was afraid she would faint. It was wrong of me, she thought, I gave too much. And she thought again, no, I was not wrong, one cannot give too much, and so I shall tell him. Oh, why does he not speak?

'Strange,' said Pagano. And he did not sound in the least angry, only bewildered. Zita opened her eyes.

'I did not know we had so many,' said Pagano.

And Zita dared to look. The cupboard was filled high with beans, a rustling golden mountain of beans.

'. . . and of such quality,' said Pagano.

'It's plain to see God loves you,' said the cook, later that day. 'If there ever was a miracle in the world, that was one.'

* * *

Time passed. Pagano's wife became ill and Zita was given the care of the children. Before long she ran the whole house. She was like one of the family, having a room of her own to sleep in, and eating at the master's table—she was more of a dear friend than a servant. And the others grudged her nothing, they had grown quite fond of her over the years and often talked among themselves of those early days when she had shamed them all with her liking for work.

'Why, she could have done everything herself,' they said, 'and still found time for her praying. What a saving the master might have made, if he had known!' And, 'Perhaps he did know. She hasn't done too badly for herself, after all.'

Then came a hard and bitter winter. The snow that had seemed so fresh and clean when it fell lay week after week in muddy ridges, thawed a little and then froze again until even the children tired of it.

In the poorer quarters of the town men died of cold, one after the other, as though struck down by plague. And still the cold continued. Zita did what she could. She took bread and soup to families in need, and comfort to the dying, but she knew that it was not enough. The poor were as many as snowflakes in the driving wind.

And now it was Christmas Eve, which should have been a time of rejoicing.

'Surely you won't go to church tonight, Zita,' said old Pagano, from his chair close to the fire. 'If you should catch your death from cold, what would become of us? And who would feed your poor?'

'They are God's poor,' said Zita. 'The food is from *your* larder, you have other servants to care for you, and yes, I am going to church.'

There was no persuading her to stay but Pagano insisted that she take his great fur cloak to keep her warm.

'And be sure you bring it back,' he said. 'If you lose it, I will throw you into the streets to live with your precious poor, d'ye hear me!'

Zita smiled and took the cloak. 'There was a time when I feared your rage,' she said, 'but I know your kind heart better now.'

'You will fear my rage again if you lose that cloak,' said Pagano.

At the entrance to the Church of San Frediano, a man stepped out of the shadows and laid his hand on Zita's arm. He was gaunt and ragged, his fingers were swollen dreadfully where the frost had bitten them, and his teeth chattered so that he could hardly speak.

'Lady,' he said, 'I beg of you. . .'

There is no coin minted that can relieve the pinch of cold and hunger late at night when neither food nor fire may be bought, but Zita had bread in her pocket and she offered that.

'Lady,' he said, 'I am . . . I am no longer . . . able to . . . eat. But the cold. The cold. . .'

As soon as she understood what it was he said, Zita unfastened her master's cloak and wrapped it about the beggar's shoulders. She kissed his icy, sunken cheek and said, 'Take this for a little while, and let me have it again when I come out of church. You see, it is not my own, but it will give you comfort for the moment and later I will find something else for you.'

She never doubted that he would wait for her, and she heard Mass with as light a heart as anyone can have, who is troubled by the wretchedness there is in the world.

As she was leaving the church, the priest said to her, 'What, Mistress Zita? Out on such a night as this in a thin dress? You will die of cold.'

And Zita answered, 'No, indeed. Good Master Pagano has lent me his fur cloak and I walk as warm as any Saracen under the hot sun.'

'Then where is it?' asked the priest.

'I lent it to a beggar at the porch,' said Zita. 'He will be waiting to give it back to me.'

'If I were a betting man I would wager San Frediano's plate that he will not,' said the priest. 'Oh, Zita, it is not necessary that a Christian should also be a fool.'

'Of course he will be waiting,' said Zita. But she was wrong. There was no sign of the beggar anywhere, and neither was there any sign of Pagano's cloak.

She went home, shivering with cold and very uneasy in her mind, to face her master's displeasure. He raged and stormed for the better part of an hour and then said, 'Well, forget it. You were always next thing to an idiot, and I should have known what to expect.'

But Zita could not forget it. She felt she had sinned twice over. She had betrayed her master's trust in her and lost him a fine rich cloak he could not easily replace—and she had put temptation in the way of a dying man. She tried to explain this to Pagano and, because he was a good man, he understood.

'If we say that the cloak was my Christmas gift to you, will that make it better?'

'It halves my sin,' she said, and wept at his generosity.

'You have the other half to bear,' he said. 'Go to bed, Zita.'

Zita prayed all night. She prayed that the beggar had

not been a thief, that he had been mistaken, that he had misunderstood, that he had supposed Pagano's magnificent cloak to be a gift.

'Oh, God, let him receive it as a gift.'

And this, not for herself, to ease her conscience, but for the sake of the beggar's soul.

'Oh, God, let him not die a thief!'

It was Pagano's custom on Christmas Day to share the feast with his servants; they would all sit down together as though they were one great family, with no difference in station between them. Pagano would carve the meat, and fill the beakers, and make long speeches about the last year and the coming one, about the state of his business and his fears for the future.

'These are hard times,' he would say, 'and they are getting worse.' And then he would lead the company in song as though he had not a care in the world, and it was true he had not many.

'This is the one day in all the year when we may be completely happy,' he would say, and then weep a little behind his hand, because he was an old man and his wife was now dead. Between anxiety, laughter and tears, the company was always a step behind him, but content to be warm and well-fed.

On this day, as usual, they were all gathered together, the master and his children, now grown and with children of their own; Zita and the cook and the manservant; the yard-man and the groom and the kitchen-maid, a twelve-year-old girl from the country, who would never be quite the treasure Zita had proved to be. And *she* was a costly treasure indeed, Pagano thought, remembering the cloak he had vowed to forget.

They were all seated, every one of them. And suddenly there was a stranger in the room, and a light as though a hundred candles had been lit at once. The stranger went to Zita and laid a rich fur cloak about her shoulders, Pagano's cloak, and smiled—then disappeared.

'How did that man get in?' cried Pagano. 'Where did he go? Who opened the door?'

No one knew. And no one had opened the door which was still bolted from the previous night. And the light, which was fading now, had yet to be explained.

Zita said, 'It was the beggar who borrowed your cloak. You see, it was not stolen after all.'

But the cook, laughing and weeping at the same time, cried, 'No. It was an angel from God.'

And Pagano remembered how strangely he had felt on the day when he sold his beans, and he remembered other things too. Surely there had been a time when a whole batch of bread had prepared itself for baking while Zita was late at her prayers. He looked at her and said, 'Many times I have been angry and unjust. Forgive me.'

Zita lived with that same family for forty-eight years. When old Pagano died she served his son and, in all those years, she never once neglected the unfortunate who revered her as the saint she was. She herself died at the age of sixty, and her body lies in the Church of San Frediano in Lucca, where the entrance is still called the Angel Door.

St. Jerome, the Lion and the Donkey

In Bethlehem, towards the end of the fourth century after the birth of Christ, a rich widow built a monastery that had a house for men, a house for women, and a third where pilgrims to the holy places might be lodged more cleanly than in the town. Here St. Jerome was to spend the last thirty-four years of his life, occupied in his great work of translating the Greek bible into Latin for the better understanding of Christians in the Roman world. Beside this undertaking, which in itself would have been sufficient labour for any ordinary man, St. Jerome continued to study Hebrew and Chaldean, to write lengthy letters on every subject that troubled the Church of his day, and to manage the business of the monastery so smoothly that it seemed to manage itself.

St. Jerome enjoyed work and hated interruptions of any kind. They were unnecessary, he said. If a duty were well explained, there should be no need to ask again concerning it; if the day were well planned, nothing could go amiss. Work was the prime necessity in life and nothing should be allowed to halt its flow.

Therefore he was not exactly pleased one morning when some of the monks, with whom he was translating a difficult text, seemed to be failing in their concentration. He spoke sharply and repeated the words he was dictating.

'What?' said one, and dropped his stylus on the floor.

The others were hastily getting to their feet and looking towards the window. One already had his leg across the sill.

'This is unseemly,' said the saint. 'I have heard no bell ring to call us from our work, and we have still a page to do. Sit down at once, brothers, and we will continue...'

'It's a lion!' said the one who had dropped his stylus. 'God knows we cannot work with a lion in the room.' And he, too, fled through the window where the others had gone before him.

'A lion! What nonsense!' said St. Jerome. 'These youngsters will be distracted by anything.'

And he took up his own pen to finish what they had abandoned. When he had written a sentence or two, he rose to consult a scroll that was lying on a shelf near the door, and then he saw that there was indeed some cause for alarm. There *was* a lion in the room—a great tawny beast with a black mane.

'This is extremely vexing,' said St. Jerome, with considerable severity in his voice. 'But I suppose you have not been among us for long enough to know that I do not care to be disturbed when I am working...'

The lion opened its wide red mouth, displaying its teeth.

'If you are hungry, you should go to the kitchens,' said St. Jerome.

The lion stayed where it stood.

'Are you deaf?' cried the saint, growing angry, and he pushed the beast, which moved aside a little and whimpered, wrinkling its muzzle. And then St. Jerome understood that the lion had not lightly interrupted his studies but had something urgent to tell him.

'Very well,' he said. 'Tell me, but tell me quickly. Life

is short and I am a busy man.'

The lion whimpered again, most dolefully, and lifted a paw for St. Jerome to see.

'So, you are hurt?'

The lion raised its huge, shaggy head and fixed its golden gaze on St. Jerome.

'You would tell me in words if you could,' said the saint. 'Come, let me see this paw.' He knelt and took the paw in his hands, gently pressing it and watching the lion's face to see where the pressure caused most discomfort. The lion winced.

'Ah, here it is,' said St. Jerome and peered closely at the soft, swollen pad. 'A thorn—and bedded deep. This will not be removed without pain, my brother, but you must have courage...'

Then, talking all the while in the most gentle and soothing way, St. Jerome took a pair of pincers from his table and set to work. Once or twice the lion growled and snatched its paw back, licking the wound and looking reproachfully at the saint.

'You must be patient, brother,' St. Jerome told him. 'I said that it would not be easy.'

At last he had it. He gave a quick, strong pull and held the thorn aloft.

'There, good fellow,' he said. 'Now I will wash and dress the wound—before long the swelling will go and you will be quite well again...'

This he did and tried to send the lion out of doors again—but the beast refused to go.

'Then stay,' said the saint. 'But I must work.'

When the young monks crept back to see if their fierce visitor had left any of the saint's bones for Christian burial, they were amazed to see St. Jerome sitting at his

desk, deeply immersed in his work, with the lion at his feet, chin on bandaged paw and purring like a kitchen cat that has tasted cream.

From that time the lion never left St. Jerome's side; when he slept it lay down by his couch; when he worked it stayed close to his desk; when he ate it sat near his stool and when he walked about the monastery it followed him as faithfully as his shadow. The holy ladies made quite a pet of it. They combed its mane and spoke soft, foolish words to it, and even slipped it extra food when they thought St. Jerome was too engrossed to notice.

But he did notice, and what he saw disquieted him.

'You are fast becoming an idle brute,' he told the lion. 'You do nothing but eat and sleep—yet every other living thing in this monastery must earn his place. Look.'

And, twisting his fingers in the lion's mane, he led it here and there about the monastery to show that this was indeed a house of industry. In the *scriptorium* monks were copying the letters of the blessed apostles; in the chapel they were chanting prayers. In the kitchen a cook was preparing the meal for the day and creating a savoury smell that made the lion's nostrils twitch; a tottering old woman was strewing herbs to sweeten the air of the dormitories; another was weeding the herb-garden. And in the apiary two figures, swathed in nets, were busy with a swarm of bees. A chained dog was barking vigorously at a pedlar in a ragged gown, and a lean brindled cat stalked across the yard from the grain-store, a rat hanging from her mouth.

'All except you are occupied, brother lion,' said St. Jerome. 'Do you intend to rest forever on the labour of these good creatures?'

The lion looked at him as though to say, 'But what can a lion do?' And truly, thought St. Jerome, a lion has few skills. When you have said that it is brave and fierce and beautiful, you have said all.

St. Jerome sat down on an upturned cask and put his mind to the question. A man who could read Chaldean as easily as Greek, and who could argue points of scholarship in Hebrew, would surely not be defeated in the problem of finding a use for a lion. . .

The sun rose higher. The old woman left the garden and took a broom to sweep, the cook brought her scoured pots into the yard to dry them in the shimmering heat, the cat went back to the granary. A hot and sweating monk came through the gateway, hauling and dragging at the bridle of a reluctant donkey. . .

'I have it,' cried St. Jerome. 'This donkey of mine has to go to the forest each day for firewood, and each day I have to send with her a man I can ill spare from other work, because the creature must be protected from wolves. Now if *you* were to keep the wolves away, Brother Paul might stay at his desk.'

The lion looked coldly at him and licked the paw that was now quite healed.

'I know what you are thinking,' said St. Jerome. 'You wish to tell me that a lion cannot load wood, but that I know. Do you take me for a fool? Brother Andreas, who is old and does not see clearly, will be glad to load the donkey, and he will do it very well although he could not defend her from a sparrow, let alone a wolf. You will look fierce and roar like thunder, and defend them both.'

So it was arranged.

Each day Brother Andreas, the lion and the donkey set out for the forest, and each day they returned together. Meanwhile St. Jerome worked at his translation and his commentaries and, at intervals, praised God for sending his donkey such a valuable guardian. All went well.

But in this world nothing continues peacefully for long. The monk, the lion and the donkey had formed the agreeable habit of sleeping a little in the heat of the day, each in his turn keeping watch. Until there came a day when, by great ill fortune, they all fell asleep together.

Each would have sworn he did no more than close his eyes for a minute—but sleep has its own laws. When brother Andreas awoke, the greater part of an hour had passed, the donkey was gone and the lion still lay sleeping, its honey-coloured belly exposed to the sun's warmth and its sides gently heaving. There was something very satisfied about its attitude and about the expression on its sleeping face—something that disturbed Brother Andreas and made him tremble.

The lion had eaten the donkey. It was obvious.

Had the poor old man been less agitated, or better sighted, he might have noticed the human foot-prints near where the donkey had been tethered, but he had only one idea in his head and he did not think of robbers. When the lion awoke, it noticed the tracks at once, and smelled the scent of strangers; it knew what had happened as clearly as though it had seen the donkey stolen but, being a beast, it could say nothing.

The old man wept and scolded and the lion hung its head for shame at having slept and so the two went sadly home to the monastery to lay the case before St. Jerome.

'I trusted you,' said St. Jerome to the lion. 'It is enough to make a man despair.'

The lion scraped the ground with its fore-paws and

turned its unhappy, glowing eyes to the saint. Every line of its sleek body suggested guilt and repentance, and St. Jerome saw this but he did not sense the true nature of the lion's shame. Such misunderstandings arise even among humankind—how much more likely between man and beast.

'Then you must take the donkey's place,' said St. Jerome. 'We cannot afford another.'

It was a fair solution. Now Brother Andreas and the lion went each day to the forest, the firewood was stacked in panniers on the lion's back, and they came home again. But it was not the happy partnership it had been. Brother Andreas no longer slept in the noonday heat for fear the lion should devour him and, deprived of his rest, grew irritable. As for the lion, it seemed that the spring had gone out of its step forever; it could not bear the reproach it saw in the eyes of those who had been its friends; it felt that even the cat despised its company. The lion's fine black mane grew matted, its coat was dull and it walked with its tasselled tail between its legs, avoiding even St. Jerome.

Winter came and the monastery celebrated Christmas but the lion would not go to the chapel to hear the singing. It remained in the donkey's old stable where it had chosen to live. There it lay with its bearded chin on its paws—and at last St. Jerome came out to comfort it.

'We are not angry with you,' said the saint. 'You obeyed your instinct rather than your reason, that's all.'

The lion twitched one ear.

'We have forgiven you,' said the saint. 'Come to the refectory and feast with us.'

The lion stirred in the straw.

'Come,' said the saint, rising to his feet. 'We cannot

manage at Christmas without our lion.'

But the lion turned its head away and looked into the distance, through and beyond the stable walls.

'Then come when you are ready,' said St. Jerome.

Spring came and still Brother Andreas and the lion went together to the forest each day, the lion plodding silently and the monk grumbling to himself.

'There is no peace in the world,' said Brother Andreas. 'In the winter it's quiet, at least, but in the spring... the traders will be round again soon with their great, clumsy-footed camels cluttering up the market-place. Spring! I'll tell you what that means! The price of everything shoots to the skies, and even the holy ladies grow restless and want to be off on pilgrimage...'

The lion halted with one paw in the air.

'Get on, do,' said Brother Andreas, and gave it a thump on the flank. 'You're even slower than that old donkey.'

But the lion did not mind. It was thinking about what the old man had said. In the spring the traders came round again...

And so it happened.

One evening a caravan of camels passed them on the road and they had to stand to one side to let it go by. The camels, laden with swords and silks from Damascus, stretched their long necks disdainfully at the dusty lion loaded with wood, and the camel-leaders in their fine woollen robes and turbans cracked their whips and shouted at Brother Andreas to get out of the way of his betters.

Behind the camels came lesser merchants with pack-mules carrying bales of cotton, and behind them again came traders in a smaller way of business, with their wares piled anyhow on the backs of donkeys.

'At this rate it will be dark by the time we get home,' complained Brother Andreas. 'You should have hurried when I told you.'

But the lion was watching the donkeys, and its eyes were glowing as they had not glowed for months.

First came a tall, gelded beast with ugly yellow teeth and a rolling eye, then a string of young females, one with a cobweb-coloured foal trotting beside her, then a sad, knock-kneed brute with a whiskery grey muzzle, and then...

The lion growled deep down in its throat and a weary little donkey with a white mask and one white leg pricked up her ears and raised her head in answer.

The lion bounded forward, still growling. Brother Andreas shouted, 'Dear God, he will kill them all!' and then closed his eyes and fell on his knees in prayer, where he remained until the tumult was over. All along the road, people were screaming and running, the camels bolted, the camel-leaders drew their short curved swords and then thought better of it and ran instead.

But the lion was not concerned with any of that. The smell of the strangers who had stolen the monastery donkey was strong in his nose—and here they were. And here was the donkey. Now St. Jerome would know the truth. He stepped slowly, stiff-legged, round the little donkey and the two men who led her, separating them from the rest of the caravan, and always keeping his face towards them, growling and showing his white teeth. His mane bristled and he lashed his tail and he drove them, the two robbers and the donkey, before him to the gateway of the monastery and through it.

St. Jerome heard a commotion in the yard, sighed and put down his pen. He wondered if perhaps his friend had now eaten Brother Andreas, and he sighed again. At this rate of progress the Church would wait for ever for his commentary on Obadiah.

'Continue with your work,' he said to the monks. 'Whatever is happening, I will deal with it.'

In the yard, Brother Paul had closed the great double-gate and was leaning against it. The robbers were alternately protesting their innocence of all knowledge of the donkey, declaring they would have the lion slaughtered and St. Jerome taken to court for abducting them, and—whenever the lion snarled—pleading for mercy and leniency, crying, 'But how could we have known it was a monastery donkey?'

'Oh, let these foolish villains go,' said St. Jerome. 'What matters most is that our donkey has been returned to us.'

Brother Paul opened the gates again though he privately thought that St. Jerome was more merciful than the occasion warranted. The two robbers crept away, and Brother Andreas came limping home, moaning, 'Alas! that lion! that lion! By this time he will have eaten a dozen donkeys—and we will have to pay...'

'He has eaten none,' said St. Jerome. 'And it is shameful that we have so misjudged him.'

He put his hand on the lion's head.

'You tried to tell me, and I would not listen. Had I treated a man so, he would have left my service long ago. But you are a brave, good beast—and a true Christian.'

Odilia and Aldaric

In the old dark days when Childeric was King of the Franks and men thought first of war, second of feasting and only third of God, there lived at Obernheim in the country of Alsace a great lord whose name was Aldaric. He was a proud, fierce man with eyes as hard and blue as sapphires in an emperor's crown; he was strong too and there was not a man in the kingdom who could lift his great iron sword, or bear the weight of his huge shield. Moreover, he had a temper that made him dangerous. Only his wife, Bereswendis, could smooth him to a show of gentleness—and there were times when even she found it better to keep out of his way than to risk his displeasure. All the same, she loved him dearly and was glad when she knew that she was going to have a child.

'It is what he needs,' she said. 'A little helpless thing to care for. It will bring out all that is good in him.'

His household, less confident, prayed that it would be so.

The midwife, who had nursed Aldaric in his infancy, and so had a special right to speak familiarly to him, said, 'My lord, I am sure this will be no ordinary child. Whether it be a boy or girl I cannot say, but there will be something about it that will open your eyes to your faults.'

Bereswendis held her breath. Surely the old woman had gone too far—but Aldaric was, for once, in a gracious mood. He laughed and answered, 'It will be a boy, of course, and he need be a strong one if he is to show *me* my faults. And if he be strong enough to do that, then he will be stronger than I am and I will be glad to learn from him.'

His wife let her breath go in a long sigh. The woman's plain-speaking had done no harm after all. He had laughed, he was happy, his goodwill might last for ever. She said, 'Of course our child will be strong. And virtuous too, I trust...'

Aldaric took her hand and kissed it. 'I will settle for strength,' he said. 'In this world it is not wise to be too virtuous.'

The child was born while Aldaric was away on his king's service—and it was a girl.

'I fear he will be disappointed,' said Bereswendis, cradling her new daughter in her arms, and indeed she feared her lord's disappointment so much that her heart pounded.

'She is a lovely child,' said the nurse indignantly. 'Any man would be proud to father such a one. She'll make a good marriage, a great alliance, and your lord will not complain about that. You'll see.'

Bereswendis tried to stifle her uneasiness. The baby was beautiful, with hair the colour of wild honey, a dark gold curling crest on her small head. Her eyes were like cornflowers and her smile was sweet and all-embracing. But she was not a boy. She would never lift her father's iron sword and swing it round her head; she would never ride, armed, to battle. These flower-petal fingers would hold nothing more deadly than a needle—and how could Aldaric bear that?

'And what shall we call the little love?' the nurse

asked, dancing the child in her arms. 'Ah, let her father choose, that's the best way.'

The weeks passed, and the baby grew in loveliness and in gaiety, charming all who came near her as though the sole purpose of her existence were to please.

'My lord will be here soon,' said Bereswendis one day. 'And of course he will love her too. . .'

In the moment of saying it she believed that it must be so, but that same night she lay sleepless thinking one moment that of course her husband would love the child—no one could fail to love such a good-humoured and affectionate baby—and the next, that if any man could so fail, then that man might well be Aldaric, who had set his heart on a warrior son.

'But we can have other children,' she told herself, 'and perhaps the next will be a son. . .' And she rose to peer into her daughter's cradle to reassure herself that all was as it should be, that this good and beautiful child would melt the hardest of hearts, would melt even Aldaric's heart.

The child lay on soft pillows, one hand resting on the fur cover, fingers curled into a tiny fist like a bud. She was awake, her blue eyes wide open, staring into the dark. Bereswendis brought the candle closer, so that the light shone full on the child's face. Her eyes did not blink, not even when the candle-flame flared in a sudden draught. Nor did they blink when Bereswendis moved her hand gently to and fro between them and the light.

'She does not know I am here,' whispered Bereswendis. And the baby heard her voice and turned towards it, smiling and reaching out her arms to be lifted.

'She is blind,' said Bereswendis. 'Dear God, she is blind.'

When they told Aldaric that his child was a girl, he said nothing. It was a blow, but it would pass. When they told him that the girl was blind, he still said nothing—but he struck the servant who brought him the news and then he took a stout lance from where it hung on the wall behind his chair and snapped it between his hands, flinging the pieces down.

Then he went to the room where his wife waited with the child in her arms. He stood in the doorway, dark with rage, and did not look at them.

'Put that brat away,' he said.

Bereswendis hesitated, trembling.

'Put it away, I said.'

Bereswendis gave her child into the nurse's care and turned back to her husband.

'My lord,' she said, her voice no louder than a breath. 'Will you not see your daughter?'

'It is not of my getting,' he said.

Many days later Bereswendis asked her husband to give the child a name. 'If you would only see her, hold her, name her, you would feel differently,' she said. 'My lord, she is as like you in looks as it is possible for a small girl-child to be like her warrior-father. Her hair is honey-gold and her eyes are blue. . .'

'It has no eyes,' he said coldly. 'It is an insult to my house, a mockery, a useless, sightless, creeping thing. I will neither see it, hold it, nor name it—you may be sure of that. Better it had never been born but, since it has been born, better it should die. Let it be drowned and then we may, in time, forget.'

Aldaric knew that he had said a terrible thing but his own pain was so great that he longed only to hurt.

'Let it be drowned,' he said again, taking a savage relish in the thought. Yet he gave no order, for not even he could be so cruel. He let Bereswendis weep a little and then he said, 'Very well, let it live—but send it away where I may never hear of it again. And send the old woman, the nurse, with it, that fool who prophesied that it would be no ordinary child...'

So the blind infant and the old woman were sent away together to a convent near Besançon, and life at the castle continued much as before, save that Bereswendis gradually pined away and died while Aldaric grew surlier in temper and more dangerous every year.

The girl thrived. In the care of her old nurse and the patient nuns she learned to weave baskets and to sew. Fine embroidery was beyond her skill but she could hem as neatly as any lady, and here her blindness was turned to advantage for she could work at night as easily as by day and her stitches never faltered as the light changed. She was a blessing on the house, as good-natured as she was beautiful, and able to laugh at her misfortune. Once she asked, 'What is my hair like? It is strange that I comb it every day, and plait it, yet I do not know what it is like.'

'It is like honey,' said her nurse, and the girl laughed.

'What? Do you mean it is sweet and sticky?'

And sometimes she would tease the nuns, making them try to describe colours to her. 'Now, red is like a rose, you say. But that is a scent, or a texture, or a shape. Is it a colour too? Yet are not some roses the colour you call yellow, and some white? So how may red be like a rose? You'll have to try again.'

She was as happy as a girl can be when she is loved, but still she had no name. She was called Girl, or Child, or Flower, or Little One, or whatever came into anyone's mind, but she had no single name that was hers alone.

When she was twelve years old the holy Erhard, Bishop of Regensberg, came to Besançon, arriving unexpectedly and throwing the convent into a turmoil.

'I had a dream,' he said, 'or perhaps a vision—I know not which. And I have come at once to obey what seemed to be a command...'

'A command?' cried the nuns. 'Concerning us?'

'That is what I believe,' said the Bishop. 'A voice came to me out of a great light and told me to ride immediately to Besançon, to baptize a child and give her the name Odilia. Have you a child here?'

The Abbess said, 'We have. And it has been a great sorrow to us that she has never been baptized, but her father, the Lord Aldaric, expressly forbade it and we have not dared to go against his will.'

'He is not a man *I* would care to cross,' said the Bishop. 'But neither may I disobey the voice that ordered me to come. I must baptize the girl and pray that her father never hears of it.'

It was not likely that he should, the nuns assured him. The man had disowned the child and never inquired about her progress.

'But we are vowed to obedience,' they said, apologetically.

'For this once, I will relieve you of it,' said the Bishop. And Aldaric's daughter was brought to him, with a white veil over her bright head, to be received into the community of Christians.

There was no preparation needed. She had been well schooled by the nuns, who had made no promises to Aldaric concerning what they taught her, and she knew how to answer the questions the Bishop asked.

He blessed the water, the holy water from the River Jordan, and touched her brow, making the sign of the cross that was both a welcome and a dedication, and gave her the name Odilia.

It is a wonderful thing to have a name, she thought. Now, when people say, 'Odilia', I shall know that they mean me. And I know who I am, Odilia.

She turned her face to the man who had given her this precious thing. She knew him as a voice in the incense-scented darkness, as a hand on her brow, as a rustling of robes and a light footfall—and now she saw him! She saw the blessed Erhard, a small man in a heavy cope; a gentle, lined face with a mouth that smiled. And she saw the ladies of the convent standing around her, and she saw her nurse, a cosy, fat body and a round face, cheeks wrinkled as an autumn apple, eyes bright with pleasure that her little one had a name at last.

'I can see!' cried Odilia. 'Blessed God, I can see!'

Then it was like a game. Odilia went from one to the other of the nuns, trying to match each face with the voice she remembered.

'No. Don't speak! Don't tell me! But you must be Sister Mechtild, and *you* must be Sister Bertha. And surely you must be Sister Gudrun. Yes, you were very strict with me when I was naughty.'

'You were never naughty,' declared Sister Gudrun, with tears of happiness running down her stern old face.

And the nurse caught Odilia in her arms and hugged her and could not bear to let her go, saying over and over again, 'If only your mother were here today. . .'

Jackdaws flew in and out through the chapel windows and added their raucous voices to the laughter. Even an inquisitive sow from the convent pig-yard came to see what the fuss was all about and, when Sister Bertha tried to chase her out, Bishop Erhard would not allow it. He said, 'Let the beasts share in our holy miracle. Besançon may never have another.'

When the excitement had died down a little, the Abbess said, 'Well, Odilia, what do you intend to do with your life? Now that you are able, you may choose for yourself.'

'I should like to be one of you,' said Odilia, quickly. 'I am happy here and no other place could mean as much to me but, dear Mother Abbess, first I must make my peace with my father.'

'I think that is not possible,' said the Abbess. 'Of course you may stay with us for ever, or for as long as you wish, but as to seeing your father. . .'

'I know that I was a bitter grief to him when I was born,' said Odilia, 'but I may be a comfort to him now. At least I should make the attempt.'

'We will write to him,' said the Abbess. 'More than that I cannot promise.'

A letter was despatched from the convent at Besançon to the castle at Obernheim and, in due course, the messenger returned.

'The Lord Aldaric received your message,' he said. 'But he will not answer it.'

'He received it,' said Odilia. 'That is a favourable sign. Please, Mother Abbess, write to him again.'

'It will do nothing,' said the Abbess, but she wrote. This time the servant brought a message back with him.

'The Lord Aldaric has no daughter. If any female claiming to be such should impose herself upon him, she will be driven away.'

'That is good,' said Odilia. 'It is almost an invitation. See, he *expects* me to go there.'

She would not be dissuaded though her nurse, the Abbess, the nuns and even the holy Bishop all tried to prevent her from going.

'If you will not send a servant with me, I will go alone,' she insisted. The Abbess gave in and provided the girl with two horses and a groom.

It was a bleak, miserable day between winter and the first awakening of spring when Odilia rode up to the castle of Obernheim and waited at the great, closed door while her servant spoke with the guard on duty there. It was a long wait and the wind was cold with sharp rain in the gusts. Odilia was tired and hungry and very much afraid, but she kept her spirits up by looking at her surroundings: at the grey stone of the castle walls, the mud on the path, the dark and gloomy trees with the rain dripping from their boughs. And as she looked, her heart sang with joy that she could see all these things.

At last her servant came back.

'It is no use, lady,' he said. 'They will not let you in.'

'Tell the man I will wait,' she said. There was no reasoning with her. He shrugged his shoulders and obeyed.

When he returned again he said, 'You had better go. The Lord Aldaric is to ride out shortly, and his man says

it will go ill with you if he should find you here.'

'A first meeting between a man and his daughter is a sacred thing,' said Odilia serenely. 'It cannot go ill. Besides, my father knows now that I am waiting for him. If he really did not wish to see me, he would stay in his hall.'

For another hour she waited. The sun came out from behind a cloud, shed a little watery light, and hid again. Her horse stamped and fidgeted, tossing his head and making small plaintive noises to show that he was bored. The groom blew on his hands to warm them and grumbled without cease.

Then, quite suddenly, the castle gate was thrown open and the Lord Aldaric came riding out, with a scattering of attendants behind him. And Odilia, with a firm mouth and trembling hands, went forward, leaving the shelter of the trees.

She saw a tall, broad man in a scarlet cloak that hung in rich folds across the flanks of the huge black horse he rode. There was gold thread on the gauntlets of his gloves, and jewels in the gold of his horse's harness, and he looked what he was—a great and powerful lord with a will that would not be gainsaid.

Odilia raised her eyes to see his face; it was like a distorted reflection of her own, seen in a pool darkened by the rank and bitter growth of overhanging weeds. Here was the same honey-coloured hair, the same blue eyes differing only in the degree of warmth in them, the same strong jaw and obstinate mouth she recognized as hers though until three months ago she had known her face only by the touch of her exploring finger-tips.

She said, 'Father...'

He passed so close that she might have touched him,

but he neither looked at her nor looked away. She turned her own horse and rode beside him, and he stared straight ahead. She quickened her pace and wheeled to block his path, smiling into his cold, unfriendly eyes—a brave stubborn girl not thirteen years old.

She said, 'My lord . . .' and he raised his whip to strike her. Her servant flinched as though he felt the lash on his own skin, but there was nothing he could do to help his lady. He said, 'Come away!' but his voice stammered between a croak and a whisper and the words sounded like nothing at all.

Odilia thought, 'He does not mean to strike but only to frighten me. Yet if I do not go, he *will* strike, for he does not like to be defied.' Even as she thought this, she was aware of the strength and beauty of her father's uplifted arm, with the grey sky behind it, as though it were no more than a pattern of shapes and textures, a glowing picture in a Book of Hours.

She said, 'I am glad to see you,' with such pleasure in her voice that all who heard it were amazed. Aldaric dropped his hand to his side. He had the air of a beast that has received its death-blow but does not yet understand what has happened.

Odilia said, 'It is true, my lord. You, who have always seen, cannot know what it is to be blind. *You* may people the darkness with remembered faces, or give an imagined form to a man of whom you know nothing other than a name, but the blind have only sounds to build on. I had heard that you were brave and strong and now I see for myself what that means. It is a miracle that is new every moment that I live.'

Aldaric said, 'What do they call you, girl?' and she answered, 'Odilia. I hope it pleases you.'

They rode back to the castle together and through the gate into the courtyard. In the hall Aldaric shouted for a room to be prepared and a feast to be made ready.

'The Lady Odilia has come home,' he said.

From that day on, it seemed he could take no step without her. She was the very hearth-place of his house, the centre of warmth and light and life. But it could not last, they were too alike for that.

Odilia reached the age of fifteen, a marriageable age, and a German Duke sent an envoy to court her on his behalf. Aldaric first said no, and said it firmly, with his fists clenched and his brows drawn together in a fierce frown. But then he thought again and the idea pleased him better. The Duke was a young man, rich, powerful and kind. He would love Odilia and protect her, and he would live longer than her father would. It was a proud alliance, one he should be glad to make—and he would not be giving up his now beloved child but sharing her.

He sent for the envoy and, with smiles and gifts, pledged his daughter to the German Duke. Then he told Odilia.

'Why, no,' she said. 'I do not intend to marry.'

It was the first disagreement between them. Aldaric stormed and raged in a way that had been forgotten for nearly three years. He brought his fist down on the massive oak table with such force that the timber split.

Odilia said, 'I am deeply sorry that you are angry, my lord father, but I do not wish to marry.'

'I do not care greatly what you wish,' said Aldaric. 'You are my daughter and you will obey me.'

'I had chosen to be a nun,' Odilia answered. 'I was happy at Besançon and willing to remain there. But because you are my father and I love you, I would have stayed with you for as long as you needed me. But if it is easy for you to part with me to a husband, it is as easy for you to return me to the convent, and there I will go.'

'You will not,' said her father. 'I did not breed you to be a mewing nun, but to give me grandsons who will hold my land.'

For five whole days they stood at loggerheads, Aldaric cursing and Odilia meek, and neither giving an inch to the other. The gentlemen of the household watched with alert, malicious eyes and made wagers among themselves as to the outcome; the servants scuttled quickly about their duties, fearing that their lord's temper would vent its spleen on them if they stayed too long within reach of his arm.

Odilia could bear it no longer. Aldaric's grief and anger was a torment to her and she would have obeyed him had it been possible. She longed to wipe out the hard lines that dragged down the corners of his mouth and to bring the laughter back to his face, but in this particular matter she could not obey. She could only remove herself from his sight—and this she did, stealing away from the castle while it slept, and going on foot so that her tracks would be more difficult to follow.

Aldaric followed her on horseback, with his hunting-dogs unleashed, determined now that she would obey him or die.

She had little hope of escape. However swiftly she ran, the dogs were fleeter and more sure of foot. The country was mountainous and where she was forced to climb painfully from rock to rock, her breath labouring, the dogs bounded with ease. She looked back and saw their lean grey shapes racing towards her, and she heard her father's horn encouraging them, and saw his red cloak, a bright point of colour among the distant trees. Panting, she leant against a rock-face, her hand pressed to her side. The dogs were so near that she could see their pink tongues and the white fire of their eyes in the sunlight . . . and she could go no further.

She cried aloud, 'Oh, dear God, help me!'

And the rock opened and let her in.

It was like being blind again, the comforting blindness of her childhood when no one had ever raised a hand to hurt her. Then she had been dependent on the kindness of the nuns whose narrow world made up the confines of her life. The space that sheltered her now was even narrower, and she was totally dependent on the love of God.

'My obstinate will was formed when I began to see,' she thought. 'Life was easier when I could only hear.'

As a child she had listened, and learned her world from sounds—voices, birdsong, the patter of rain on dry ground. In the rock she listened again and heard the music of deep silence. And then she heard her father weeping. This was something more for her to learn and, in the dark of the earth, she learned it, that it is good to have a will of one's own but sometimes better to put it to one side or to give it up to a greater good.

'Please, God, let me out,' she whispered. 'Let me out so that my father may forgive me—if he wishes.'

The rock opened at once and Odilia stepped into the bright day, from blindness to sight as on the day of her baptism. But this time she held her will in check and stood with her head bowed, waiting for what would happen.

Aldaric bowed his head too, and told her that he had

been wrong, that all his dealings with her had been wrong, that he had been blind all his life—yes, and deaf too—because of his pride.

'It costs me something to admit it,' he said. 'But a man's faults are like the skin of a snake. They fit tightly yet may be sloughed off. So be a nun, if your heart is set on it. But stay here, do not go back to Besançon.'

He gave her his castle of Hohenberg for a convent and, because it was built high among the rocks and difficult to reach, he also gave her land on the plain below where she built a refuge for the sick and a hostel for pilgrims.

All this happened many centuries ago, but a statue of Saint Odilia still stands on the Hohenberg, which is now called Odilienberg, and her shrine is still a place of pilgrimage, especially for the blind.

St. Moling and the Fox

St. Moling had a way with beasts and a sore trouble it was, at times, to those about him. A monk might be milking a cow in the long pasture down by the stream when the creature would suddenly take it into her head that she wanted to hear St. Moling preach and, without warning, would kick over the bucket and be off, leaving the monk sitting on his stool with his head in his hands and thoughts in his heart that were not very much like prayers. Or another would spend the whole morning getting the pigs together and driving them into the woods to forage, and then be bowled over and flattened to the ground by their headlong stampede to get back to the monastery when they heard St. Moling's bell.

Indeed, the monks said there were days when they couldn't get near St. Moling for beasts, and few men can keep their minds on spiritual matters when a wolf is nudging them. For it was not only the domestic animals that crouched at the saint's feet to hear him, but wild creatures from the woods and hills—stags that trampled the corn on their way to and from the monastery, shaggy-coated wolves, badgers and slender stoats with their ears listening to St. Moling's words about brotherly love while their shining eyes were fixed on the rabbits who nestled as near to the speaker as they could get.

There was a fox too, a fine russet-coloured gentleman

with a snowy chest and delicate-stepping black legs. This one had a lair in the woods where he kept his vixen and cubs, but he spent most of his time with the monks, regarding the monastery as his second home.

'It is a heavy cross we have to bear,' said one brother to another as they collapsed together on a bench after chasing a furious, spitting wild-cat from the dairy.

But St. Moling would not hear of their setting snares.

'We are all God's children,' said the saint. 'They, as well as ourselves, have the right to share his blessing.'

'I am willing enough to share God's *blessing* with a badger,' said one, 'but I am less willing to share my bed with it. And as for that fox. . .'

No one, save St. Moling, really trusted the fox. And no one was surprised when he stole a hen from the hen-run and ate it, careless of who might be watching; he even sauntered into the chapel with feathers clinging to his muzzle. This was something the saint could not overlook.

He spoke severely to the fox, who heard him with an air of outraged innocence. Hens, the fox reasoned, were designed to be eaten, as foxes were designed to eat them. Here was nothing to warrant such a fuss and bother. But when the saint wept for grief that the fox had so betrayed his trust, the creature hung his head and looked ashamed. Such sorrow might be foolish and unjustified but it deserved respect.

'Somehow I must make amends,' thought the fox, and he ran quickly through the woods to a convent of holy women that was situated on the other side. But these women, he found, were stricter in their ways than the monks; it was not so easy to get into *their* hen-yard.

'This needs strategy,' thought the fox and, by means

of certain terrible threats, he managed to enlist the help of a mouse who was set to create a diversion while he carried out his raid.

The mouse did all that was expected of him, he was like a dog in a field of sheep. The holy women ran hither and thither, holding up their skirts and leaping on to benches and chairs while the mouse alternately hid and showed himself to keep them scurrying.

Meanwhile the fox crept into the hen-yard unobserved, selected a fat brown hen and took her by the neck, but gently. The hen did not struggle at all; she gave one small choked squawk and gave herself up, a picture of resignation.

St. Moling was in the *scriptorium*, painting birds and flowers in the margins of a Gospel book, when the fox came in and laid the hen at his feet as if to say, 'Master, here is a fowl to replace the one I ate.'

The saint guessed at once where he had got it and said, 'Miserable animal, this too is theft. Do you think you can make something right by adding wrong to wrong?'

It seemed to the fox that certain people were very hard to please, and he was tempted to eat this hen, too, and hear what the saint would say to that—but then it occurred to him that his master's voice was tender.

'Take the bird back where you found it,' said St. Moling, with the slightest of stresses on the word *found*. 'I think you meant well, so I will give you the benefit of the doubt as to your methods. But if I ever catch you with a hen between your jaws again. . .'

He turned back to his work, sketching the head of a crafty fox among the acanthus leaves.

So the fox took the hen back to the convent where she settled down again, only a little the worse for her adventure, inclined to moult and go broody with no good cause, but otherwise unharmed. He had had his trouble for nothing.

'You cannot make a Christian out of a fox,' said one of the monks to St. Moling. 'Nature is too strong in him, and it will always break out.'

'So it is with many men,' said the saint. 'Yet we continue to struggle on their behalf. And think, brother, this creature understood my words and obeyed them, which is one of the wonders of the world. He has made a good beginning.'

Now, whenever St. Moling worked in the *scriptorium* the fox sat with him, and the saint would talk seriously to him about the necessity of leading a virtuous life, much of which went over the fox's head. What is virtuous in a man is not always so in a beast.

But he was an intelligent animal and, when he heard about the reward that virtue gained in heaven, he thought he knew what was meant—an unlimited provision of geese, ducks and hens, and no nonsense about rightful ownership.

'Well and good,' thought the fox. 'I would like to earn such a reward as that, but how may virtue be acquired?' St. Moling droned on about kindness and generosity, forgiveness and self-denial and even about prayer and fasting, but none of these holds a large place in a fox's life, and the saint could not know what was passing through the mind of his elegant bushy-tailed friend.

'This virtue—whatever it may be—must be hidden in these books,' thought the fox. 'Why otherwise should my master devote so much time to them when, by his own account, virtue is the most desirable thing in the world, the thing most worth pursuing?'

So he began to give some attention to the vellum pages strewn on St. Moling's desk. The curious black marks, some straight, some curved and some round, puzzled him. They were the same and yet not the same, and they used up much of the space. But the little pictures in the margins he *could* recognize—fat tumbling rabbits, crowing roosters, pigs and calves and the kitchen cat. And ever and again he found himself portrayed, peering from behind a wall, racing across the head of a page, or sitting, with his tail tucked neatly round his feet, in the centre of an initial letter.

It was quite obvious to him that he was the main subject of St. Moling's book, and that the lesser beasts and birds were his reward. As for the strange black marks, perhaps *they* were the virtue St. Moling praised so highly, the virtue he must acquire before gaining the reward? He rasped them with his tongue and the ink had a bitter taste.

Unfortunately he was unable to satisfy his appetite for virtue there and then, for at that moment the saint came in and carried away the pages to be bound between stout covers. The fox went too and, during the next few days, kept a careful watch on the proceedings, taking particular note of the shelf where the finished book was laid.

Next he had only to wait until all the brothers were occupied elsewhere, and then to act with speed. He sprang to the shelf, snatched up the book in his teeth, and made off with it to his lair in the woods where he would be able to devour it at his leisure. Or so he thought.

But the book was missed almost immediately, and St.

Moling, though a patient, easy-going man, was no fool. He guessed at once that the fox was the culprit, caught him by the scruff of his neck as he strolled through the cloisters and carried him off to the *scriptorium* to have the matter out.

For a full hour he lectured the fox, who listened at first with astonishment and then with indignation. Indeed he had been told before, and many times, that it was wrong to steal—but those had been occasions concerning hens and he had been caught with feathers round his mouth. Who had seen him take the book? Truly, the minds of men were beyond his understanding.

At last St. Moling let him go and, in a very little while, he returned, bringing the book with him, the pages only a little loose and gnawed where the cubs had been having a game with it.

'You are forgiven,' said the saint. 'But woe betide you if you ever touch a book again. Now be off with you.'

And the fox never did touch another book, which the saint regarded as a sign of true repentence.

'See how wrongly you have judged our brother fox,' he told the monks. 'You would have beaten him for his crimes and driven him away as an outcast. But *I* spoke firmly to him, pointing out his errors, which he understood. And thus have I brought him round to virtue...'

As for the fox, he was among the bee-hives. He had stolen a honeycomb and now he was licking his fur clean—but that was something St. Moling did not know.

The Farm-Labourer Who Wanted to See Jerusalem

There are few men without ambition of one sort or another—whether it be for wealth or power or holiness, a horse or a new cloak or a house with a garden that overlooks the sea.

Isidore was ambitious to see Jerusalem. It was a small longing compared with that of a man who sets out to make himself emperor but, for someone in Isidore's position, it was just as hard to achieve.

He was a farm-labourer. He rose before dawn and went to bed at dusk, and all the hours between were spent ploughing, sowing, reaping, baling—and then preparing the ground again for another harvest. But it was good labour, and Isidore would have chosen no other. He saw God's hand at work in the soil, drawing the green stems from the seed, and washing the fields with the gold of ripening grain; he saw God's blessing in the sun and his mercy in the rain and his bounty in the loaded carts that bore the harvest away.

But when he talked about these things to his fellow labourers, they grew impatient with him. It was work, they said, and no more than that. It meant aching backs and stiff muscles, parched throats and the fear of famine.

'And it's the master gets the profit,' they said. 'It's him that'll get to Jerusalem, not you.'

They thought him a fool, and worse than a fool, to think so much of God.

'Look,' they said. 'A man works hard all the week and fills his belly as well as he can. But no one wants to be damned—we'll grant you that—so on Sunday he goes to church and hears Mass. That takes care of his soul. What's the point of hearing Mass every morning, particularly if it means rising an hour earlier? You'd be better off in bed, man, saving your strength for the day. And in the evenings too—why bend your knees in the church when you might be bending your elbows at the tavern?'

'It is the way God made me,' said Isidore.

That was all very well, but if Isidore stayed late in the church among the candles and the crosses, he was late in getting to the fields—and that made trouble. The workmen went to John de Vergas, their master, and complained.

'So it means that you have to do his work as well as your own,' said the master. 'That is bad, I agree.'

This made the men uncomfortable, for not one of them could remember ever having had to reap so much as a single sheaf for Isidore, though they all knew that he had more than once stayed late to help them with their own work when they had rested too long at midday.

'He is always behind us, starting,' they said.

John de Vergas was not the sort of master to reprimand a man on nothing more than the word of another, so the next day he went to the fields to see for himself if what they said about Isidore were true.

And indeed, there were the men ready to plough, with their oxen harnessed, and the birds gathering for worms they would find in the furrows, but there was no sign of Isidore.

The ploughing was already well underway when he

appeared, not even hurrying.

'Why, this is brazen,' thought de Vergas, and he started forward to speak his mind. But he went no further than a step. . .

There was something very strange about this field, about the air above it. It seemed to be filled with movement—as though invisible shapes shifted and shifted again, displacing the air—and yet there was nothing to be seen.

'A trick of the wind,' he muttered. But there was no wind.

'There's something wrong with my eyes,' he told himself. 'I worked too late last night by candle-light, and now I am paying for it.'

But there was nothing wrong with his eyes. He could see the other fields quite plainly, with the oxen plodding ahead, the men guiding the heavy ploughs. He could even see the dry top-soil trickling back into the new-made furrows, and separate grass-blades and the fine threads of roots.

And in the near field, he could see Isidore walking like a man in a dream—and almost half the field had been ploughed. But he could not be sure, the light was leaping so. De Vergas closed his eyes a moment and then looked again, not at Isidore but beyond him, at the light. And he saw a second team of oxen, white as summer clouds, with two men driving them. Two men! They were taller than any man de Vergas had ever seen, and they were not girded for plough-work, but robed like the stone saints in the church he attended in Madrid. Furthermore their shadows were a brightness that made the sun itself look dark.

Isidore reached the end of the field, turned and came

slowly back. He was enjoying the smell of the fresh-turned earth, and the warmth of the risen sun on his shoulders, and thinking what a fine day God had provided for the ploughing—all these things at once—when he saw his master waiting. He quickened his step, for it would not do to keep such an important man standing about as though he were a village lad.

'Do you wish to speak to me, master?' he called.

'Aye,' said de Vergas, though he no longer knew what he wanted to say.

Isidore came up and stood quietly, with his cap in his hand, while de Vergas watched the angels reach the far end of the field and dissolve in their own light.

'Yes,' he said. 'When next you are in church, will you say a prayer for me?'

And Isidore did not think it odd that a busy man should leave his counting-house in the morning for the sole purpose of asking a farm-servant to pray for him. He said, 'Gladly, master,' and turned back to his work.

Side by side with his love of God and his love of work, Isidore loved beasts and birds. He cared for his ox's comfort as though it were his own, and never drove him beyond the limit of weariness as some other men did; he loved his dog's bounding welcome at the end of each day, and the thrust of the damp muzzle against his palm. This was another thing that set him apart from his fellows.

'Look,' they said. 'An ox is an ox. When he's dead, he's so much meat and leather, and while he lives, he works. You've no sense when it comes to beasts, man. And it's the same with birds. You save your crumbs to feed them, but what has a bird ever done for a man?'

'I have heard that ravens fed the prophets in the desert,' said Isidore, after some thought. But they shrugged and said that was something else, a different matter; such things did not happen nowadays.

'You must be reasonable,' they told him. 'If you think of nothing but miracles, you'll forget what you are doing and find yourself in trouble.'

In fact Isidore never gave a thought to miracles. Though he fed the birds, he expected no return; it was enough simply to see them fly and to hear their singing. For that it would be worth giving up his whole dinner, not only the crumbs of it. And winter was a bad time for birds.

There came a day when he and Pedro, another man from the farm, were carrying a sack of corn to be ground at the mill.

'It's a bad day to be out, whatever the purpose,' Pedro growled. 'Moreover, the miller won't stir till the sun comes up—and no more would I!'

It was bitter weather. Snow lay in drifts like great goose-feather pillows all along the track and against the low stone walls. The sky was heavy and yellow and full of snow.

Isidore did not answer at once. He was looking at a tree ahead and wondering what kind of tree it could be that still had leaves on its branches.

'Do you see?' he asked. 'Every other tree we have passed is bare . . . but look at that.'

They drew closer and Pedro said, 'Those aren't leaves, you fool. They're some of your precious birds—and, by God, enough to make a fair meal—if only we had a net.'

'Poor birds,' said Isidore. 'The berries must have

failed this winter, or be hidden so deep under the snow that it needs more than a beak to find them.'

One fluttered to his hand and he held it, stroking its breast with his thumb. ''Tis nothing but feather and bone,' he said. 'Not even you, Pedro, could make a meal of these.'

'Come on,' said Pedro. 'This corn is heavy, and the sack has frozen to my shoulders. You must take your turn with it now.'

'Corn!' cried Isidore, as though he had not known what they were carrying. 'Corn! Why Pedro, this is Providence!'

'Whatever it is, you carry it,' said Pedro.

'We will feed the birds,' said Isidore, taking hold of the sack. But now Pedro was reluctant to part with it.

'Not with our master's corn,' he said.

'It is God's corn,' said Isidore firmly. 'He made the seed, and sent the rain to wet it, and the sun to ripen it. He would not wish his birds to starve.'

And he took the sack by force, opened it and poured out a heap of corn—a half and more than a half of what the sack had held.

'I'll have nothing to do with it,' said Pedro. 'You take the sack, half-empty as it is, and you take the blame. It will serve you right if you are whipped for the madman you are and turned away from your place. What's more, I'll wager a beaker of wine against a crust of bread that there isn't a bird in the sky that will help you out of your trouble.'

But he went on with Isidore to the mill, he wanted to see the end of the tale, and hear what Isidore would say to the miller.

The miller took the sack and weighed it in his hands.

'Hardly worth bringing so little,' he said. 'And so far. And on such a day. Is this all your master could spare from the harvest?'

'It is all we brought with us,' said Pedro, scowling.

But when the sack was emptied into the scales, there was more corn poured out than had ever before been carried in one, two, or even three sacks, and the miller had to fetch more weights to set in the balance before the scale would tip.

People now began to look at Isidore more respectfully. There was more to him, they felt, than met the eye. Pedro spoke in a hushed voice of what he had seen at the mill, and some others among them had glimpsed the angelic ploughmen, and others again had heard—though they had not seen for themselves—that Isidore had, more than once, fed a whole host of beggars with a crust of bread and a handful of beans.

Nevertheless they still laughed when he spoke of Jerusalem, and his great desire to go there. They were able to laugh at this because it was something they understood. Jerusalem, though very far away, was a real place in the world they knew; it was a city any ordinary man might visit, if he were rich enough. The idea of a labourer actually making such a journey was absurd, for in those days, when a farm-worker received the greater part of his wages in the produce of the land, there was little he could put aside in the way of silver.

But whatever Isidore could manage to save, he did. Whenever he ate bread instead of meat, and drank water instead of wine, he said to himself, 'I am a step or two nearer Jerusalem. . .'

That was how he thought of it—one step at a time.

And his small hoard, his Jerusalem money, grew until it represented a considerable number of steps. It began to seem possible that one day, before he died, he would indeed see the Holy City.

One night he was sitting alone in his room, planning the journey in his mind as he often did, and deciding what he would see first, when there came a knock at the door. There was nothing unusual in this, for winter often brought benighted travellers to his house, and he was glad to welcome them.

And there was nothing unusual in this visitor, except that he looked too old and frail a pilgrim to be abroad alone at night, and in such an inclement season.

Isidore brought him to the fire, and stirred it up, and added more wood to make a blaze. More wood so late in the evening meant a step back, not forward, but a guest must be warmed and fed, whatever the cost.

So Isidore shared his warmth and his supper, and then leaned closer to hear what the traveller had to say about the world he had seen.

'I see you have been in Compostella,' said Isidore, for the old pilgrim carried a cockle-shell in the band of his broad-brimmed hat.

'Yes,' said the pilgrim. 'I have been there. I have been to Rome too, and many other places. I saw the cell where the blessed Peter lay in chains. I have seen the phial of Christ's dear blood in Mantua.' He sighed heavily. 'And I have seen Jerusalem...'

'Sweet God,' said Isidore, scarcely breathing.

'I have been everywhere,' said the pilgrim. 'I have seen everything there is to see—and now I am going home...'

And he began to weep, rocking backwards and

forwards, the tears running down his cheeks into his beard.

'There may be no one left to welcome me,' he said.

'Tell me about it,' said Isidore. He had longed to hear about Rome, and Mantua, and Compostella; above all he had longed to hear about Jerusalem but, instead, he listened while the old man spoke of his own home in the north, the fine house he had lived in, with the orchard behind it, and the stream where he had fished as a boy.

'And I may never see it again,' said the old man. 'It is too far, and I have no money for the journey. I shall die on the road, and all my wandering will have come to nothing.'

'To have seen the holy places,' said Isidore, 'that is something.'

'But not enough! may God forgive the blasphemy! I had a wife once, and a son, and I do not know if they are still alive. Can you understand what that means to an old man?'

'I would understand it if I could,' said Isidore, 'but it is not easy to get inside another man's grief. I feel for you, yet even while I feel for you, my mind says, "This man has seen Jerusalem!"'

That was true while he said it. But another thought was growing in his mind. He looked at the pilgrim and saw that he was indeed near death, his faded eyes already focused on another world, and that it was only the will to die in his own country that forced him on.

'I have money,' Isidore said. 'No, don't speak yet, listen. I have a little money saved, not enough to take me to Jerusalem, but enough to get you home. It is yours, take it.'

He took the worn leather wallet from its safe place

under his mattress and put it in the pilgrim's hand.

'I will pray for your safe journey,' he said, and felt as though his heart would break.

The old man took the wallet and said nothing, but the wonder in his face spoke of much.

'Sleep now,' said Isidore. 'Have my mattress and sleep well.'

Isidore sat until the fire died, and then he sat for a long while in the dark, waiting for the numbness to leave the place where he thought his heart must be. This is not regret, he said to himself, for I have done what it was right to do. It was for this that I saved my Jerusalem money, and for nothing else. But somehow I have lost direction...

He grew restless and longed for some occupation for his hands, wishing that morning would soon come and he could work again. That would be better, the new day would bring relief.

He crossed the room and opened the door upon the night. There was no hint of dawn in the sky; even the fields slept. But as he looked, the world seemed to tilt about him. He staggered and put out his hand to steady himself against the doorpost—but there was only an emptiness where his house had stood, and a rushing wind...

And Isidore found himself walking through strange fields on a hillside in the heat of noon.

A voice said, 'Are you afraid, Isidore? Surely not. These are the fields above Bethlehem, where long ago an angel appeared to a group of wandering shepherds.'

Isidore turned to see who spoke, but the light dazzled his eyes. Certainly there seemed to be a figure at his shoulder, but at the same time and in the same space the figure occupied, he could see the grass and wild flowers and the line where the top of the hill touched the sky. There was no one with him—yet he had an impression of sandalled feet, and a white robe, an old broad-brimmed hat with a cockle-shell in its band, and a stout staff. And great, spreading wings. The voice said, 'Come. I will show you Jerusalem.'

And Isidore saw the holy places—Nazareth and the River Jordan and the Lake of Gennesaret where Christ had taught the people from a fishing boat. And he saw Capernaum where Peter's wife's mother had been cured of a fever, and Nain where the widow's son was raised from the dead. And at last he saw Jerusalem and—this was strange—he saw it as it had appeared in Christ's own day, with the great temple standing. He saw the merchants and money-changers in the Court of the Gentiles, and heard the interpreters of the Law disputing among themselves about the meaning of truth and neighbourliness.

His guide seemed to shuffle time as though it were a pack of cards for, when Isidore looked again, the temple was fallen save for its great wall, and there were pilgrims in the streets, and Christian shrines.

On the Mount of Olives he saw the church that the Emperor Constantine had built to mark the site where Christ had foretold the destruction of the city and, coming down from there, he walked in the Garden of Gethsemane, thinking he must be in a dream.

He saw the coloured pavement where Pilate had sat in judgement, and he followed the road to Calvary, the place of the skull, where he thought he saw three crosses sharp against a lowering sky—in a place where the hill was bare and the sky above it blue.

They stood once more in the fields above Bethlehem and the guide said, 'You have seen all that you wished to see. Will you remember it?'

'How should I ever forget?' said Isidore.

'I will see that you do not,' said the guide, and he took Isidore's hand and struck him on the palm.

And Isidore, shocked by the sudden pain, put out his other hand to steady himself—and there, behind him, was the door of his house. This time there was no tilting of the world, no rushing wind, to mark the passage from one space to another, but one moment the light and heat of Palestine and the next, the darkness of a Spanish night and the cold of winter. That was all.

He went into his house and he might have been returning from any small journey, perhaps from Madrid where he sometimes went on feast-days; he had the same sense of coming home to a quiet, empty house. The blanket on his mattress was tumbled, but there was no sign of the pilgrim.

'Was he a pilgrim or an angel?' Isidore asked aloud. Well, whoever or whatever he had been, the purse of money had gone with him.

Then Isidore slept.

His first thought on waking was that he had had a wonderful dream, something to tell the priest. He was arranging the words in his mind when a sudden, stabbing pain made him look at his hand—and there were blue marks on the palm which he could not rub away, though he spat and rubbed until his skin tingled.

'These marks are like letters,' he said, and went to ask his master what they could mean.

John de Vergas looked long at Isidore's hand, and listened to his story. He remembered the angels who had ploughed his field so many years before and he knew that once again he was in the presence of a holy mystery.

'I do not know what they mean, Isidore,' he said. 'But we will ask the priest.'

The priest peered closely and turned Isidore's hand this way and that. 'Yes, here is something written,' he said at last. 'It may be Hebrew, but I am no scholar and I can't be sure.'

'Then we will go to Madrid,' said John de Vergas. 'I know a Jew there who will read it for us, if indeed it is Hebrew.'

Isidore hesitated.

'He is an honest man,' said de Vergas, not understanding. 'I do business with him and, I assure you, he has never tried to cheat me. . .'

'I have no fear of that, master,' said Isidore. 'But I am already late for work. There is wood to be cut and stacked, and I intended to mend the gate today, that the black bull broke a month ago.'

'Come,' said de Vergas. 'We will go to Madrid.'

The Jew welcomed Isidore and his master. He gave them wine, and biscuits that tasted of almonds, and then he said, 'Well now, let me look at this writing in your hand, this writing that your priest cannot read.'

Isidore held out his hand for the third time that day, but in his heart he felt he already knew what the Jew would tell him. He thought that perhaps de Vergas knew it too, had known it from the first—this visit to Madrid was necessary not only to confirm what they both suspected, but to set the moment of their knowing apart from the common day, that its significance should not be marred.

The Jew took Isidore's hand in his.

'You will not tell me how the writing came there?' he asked.

'Not yet,' said de Vergas. 'But if you can tell us what these letters mean, we will tell you then.'

'My part is easily done,' said the Jew. 'The writing is Hebrew, as you guessed. The characters are excellently formed and, I would say, not written by a common scribe...'

'It was no common scribe, certainly,' said Isidore.

The Jew folded Isidore's fingers over the writing on his palm.

'Do you need me to tell you that the word is Jerusalem?' he said.

St. George and the Dragon

In many ancient books Libya is all that part of Africa which is not Egypt—and we may only guess where the city of Silene stood. Yet it was here, they say, that St. George killed a dragon and rescued a princess.

This is how it happened.

There was very little for a soldier to do in Silene. He might drink himself insensible on the dark, sweet Libyan wine they sold in the Old City, or he might try his fortune at dice—but young George, when new to the service, had lost a month's pay in advance on a single throw, and somehow his taste for gambling had gone with it.

So he took to riding out alone on his good army horse, to take a look at the country. He wondered what it would be like to live there, to be a part of it. Sometimes he toyed with the idea of leaving the service altogether, marrying a local girl and settling down. But he found the people hard to know. True, they were polite enough, but they never let him forget that he was a tribune in the army of occupation. To them he was Rome, the oppressor, an alien foot on their land. They called him sir, and sold him fodder for his beasts at a price that seemed reasonable, but they never sent for their wives and daughters to meet him and they never invited him into their houses.

In the beginning he had tried to cross the barrier. He

had said, 'All right—so I'm a tribune in the Roman army. But that need not make me an enemy. And I am not a Roman. . .'

And the soft-voiced man had said, 'Indeed, sir?' without interest, and returned to the bargain he was driving.

George's brother officers considered him a fool for making the attempt. There was no need to know the country, nor to be on friendly terms with the people. Soldiering was an occupation, no more than that.

They said, 'Do you expect a tax-collector to be popular?' and laughed.

But George was a Christian, born of Christian parents, and that, they felt, made a difference. George felt it too.

He said, 'These people are my fellow men,' and was pained when an old veteran struck him on the shoulder and said, 'Then your fellow man would put a knife between your ribs, given half a chance and a dark night.'

'That is not the way a Christian looks at it,' said George.

Now, having a few days' leave in hand, he took a sack of provisions and a bed-roll behind him in the saddle, and turned his horse's head towards the desert. He had some vague notion of proving—to himself if to no one else—that he could be respected as a man and a hero, not because he had Rome behind him, but in his own right. How this might be achieved he did not know, but meanwhile it was a fine thing to eat and sleep under the stars and to wake slowly in the gathering light, wash in spring water, and ride on again with the reins slack in his hands.

He neither knew nor cared where he went and he had the sun for company—the same sun that shone on his own home near the Aegean Sea. That was hard to believe, but it was true. Dear God, how he missed the Aegean.

And on some days the desert shimmered like the sea, but the sky was white and the sun a blazing ball. That was a punishing sun. It reminded him that he had no real place in Libya.

Sometimes there was a breeze from the north, blowing off the Mediterranean, he supposed. Then his spirits rose and he whistled like a bird, forgetting his loneliness. But, for the most part, the silence was oppressive.

To break the silence, George talked to his horse. He spoke of all he could remember of his childhood, and of the old stories his grandmother had told him in the lamplight—tales of heroes and monsters and magical islands that sank beneath the ocean. He had loved those stories, but his parents had said they were all nonsense, and forbidden them.

The horse listened and moved his ears. He was glad to hear his rider's voice, for the silence made him nervous. Then George told him about the girl he had loved.

'She was very beautiful,' he said. 'She had dark hair and eyes and. . .' He found he could not remember her very well.

'. . . she was amazingly beautiful.'

Two or three days later he was still struggling to remember her, and to explain to his horse what this wonderful girl had meant to him.

'I never dared to speak to her,' he said, 'so of course she married someone else . . . possibly a Roman. And then she was forbidden, you see, like my grandmother's stories...' He found that he was weeping.

'So I joined the army ... the Roman army ...' He slumped forward in the saddle, caught himself falling asleep and jerked upright again.

'Although I am not a Roman,' he said, with great firmness.

Then, wide awake, he saw he was being foolish, talking like that to a dumb beast, and he knew it was time to return to Silene before he became quite unmanned by his loneliness. He suspected too that he had already overstayed his leave—and that was a serious matter in the Roman army. Of course, he reasoned, he could tell them he had lost his way...

And so he had.

In panic he turned his horse about, and about again, as he searched for a landmark that might guide him. But the wilderness offered no help at all; one thorn bush is very like another. He could no longer remember whether he had ridden towards the setting sun or away from it; he could not tell whether that bright star just rising above the horizon had been on his left or on his right.

There was nothing he could do but ride straight on. Perhaps the horse's sense would lead them home, horses were wiser than men about such things.

George clicked his tongue and the horse tossed his head in answer, and set off at a steady pace. Yes, he knew what was expected of him.

The sun goes down quickly in that part of the world and soon it was quite dark, but the horse seemed both sure and tireless. Sometimes his hooves rang on stone as though they travelled a road—a good Roman road—and then after a while the sound was muffled again by dust.

Gradually his pace slackened to a careful walk. He went slowly and haltingly and at last stopped altogether. George rolled from the saddle and slept where he fell, only dimly aware of the prickle of coarse grass against his cheek, and of a curious rank smell he could not trouble himself to identify.

He slept till the sun roused him. The smell was still strong in his nostrils, and he saw that his horse had brought him to the edge of a wide marsh, a nightmare place of reeds and water and oozing mud with here and there a causeway half-built and already rotting.

He also saw a comely, dark-faced man who leaned on a spear, watching him.

George climbed awkwardly to his feet.

'I am a Roman officer. . .' he began. But the dark-faced warrior evidently had no respect for Rome. He prodded George with his spear and said, 'You had better come to the King.'

It is never wise to argue with a man who has a spear in his hand, so George went with him, and the horse followed.

The King's village stood on slightly higher ground, and the marsh was hidden from it by a high wall of plaited reeds plastered with mud. The houses were made of mud too, but were well built and spacious. Beyond the village on its landward side were fields of grass, knee-high and of a rich green. At first sight it was a prosperous-seeming place but there was something about it that was wrong, that made the hair rise at the nape of George's neck. Perhaps it was the silence, or the sadness on the faces of the people who came out to see them pass, or the fact that there were no animals—

neither sheep nor cattle in the fields, nor goats, nor even a solitary dog roaming the long street between the houses.

Or perhaps it was the stench that hung in the air. That in itself was wrong.

George was led to the King's house and into the King's presence.

'I am a Roman officer...' he began. But the King seemed to care no more for Rome than had his watchman. Could it be possible that they had never heard of Rome?

'We do not care greatly who you are,' said the King. 'It merely grieves us that we cannot welcome you as we once welcomed strangers. You find us in an unhappy hour.'

'Tell me,' said George, simply.

And, while the people fidgeted and peered anxiously through the open door to watch the progress of the sun, the King told him.

It seemed that they were the remnant of a once noble nation, brought to extreme need by the voracious habits of a dragon.

'That stinking marsh', said the King, 'was once a lake. The dragon has fouled it with his breath, as he has fouled the very air, and fouled our lives.'

At first the brute had been appeased by gifts of sheep and cattle, which he had devoured whole—fleece and hide, flesh, bone and entrails. But the time came when there were no more herds and not a single, bleating lamb.

'So we looked to our maidens to save us,' said the King. 'What else could we do?'

They had chosen the maidens by lot.

'It seemed most just,' said the King, 'though some thought it more sensible to send the plumpest first. . .'

'I doubt it would have made any difference in the end,' said George.

The dragon had accepted the change of diet—one maiden every day, neither more nor less—and each morning, at first light, the lot was drawn and the chosen maiden, robed in white and garlanded with flowers like a spring sacrifice, was rowed out to an island in the swamp, and left there until the dragon's belly told him it was time to feast.

'Today it is my own daughter's turn,' said the King.

'Did you never think of killing the dragon?' asked George. It seemed to him that these people had given in very easily.

'It is impossible,' said the King. 'Several of our young men have tried it—but the beast will only leave the swamp for a tethered maiden. There is nothing we can do but mourn.'

George heard himself saying, 'I will kill your dragon. It was for this that my horse brought me here.'

'If you succeed,' said the King, 'you may marry my daughter and rule my people after me. Whoever you are and wherever you come from, I can see that you are a man.'

George thought very quickly. If he killed the dragon and married the lady, he would be gaining a new people for the Empire. Perhaps Rome would even overlook the fact that he was an officer who had overstayed his leave; it seemed his adventure might end very well.

Then it struck him that giving another nation for Rome to swallow was like giving another maiden to the dragon. Where did the difference lie?

He said, 'If I kill the dragon, it will be with Christ's help.'

And the King said, 'Who is Christ?'

'He is my God,' said George. 'If I kill the dragon, will you undertake to worship him as I do?'

'We will indeed,' said the King. 'For this is something our own gods have failed to do. Perhaps your god is more powerful than they are and, that being so, more worthy of our worship.'

So George was rowed out to the island with his horse. He was given a lance and left there to wait for whatever would happen, and he was terribly afraid.

When he and the princess were alone together, he said, 'This lance looks a very little thing to use against a monster that can swallow an ox at one gulp—I think we had better pray.'

And he taught the princess to pray too, while the horse just nibbled the grass.

When they had waited for perhaps an hour, the water of the marsh began to shiver along the surface, and then to bubble and boil as though a fire had been lit underneath. The dreadful stench intensified.

'I think the end will come quickly now,' said George, and he hoped that he was speaking of the dragon's end. He called to his horse and mounted. The princess handed him the lance.

And then the water appeared to part, falling away on two sides to reveal first a long, ugly snout, low brow and wicked eyes, then a long, scaly back all slimy from the swamp-bed, dripping with stinking weed, and then a long, barbed tail that lashed the sluggish water into foam.

The monster gaped, showing all its fearful teeth, and streams of saliva fell hissing on to its clawed feet.

It bellowed, and the horse started to dance and rear as though he were jerked on strings. The princess moaned and closed her eyes, but she did not stop praying. George prayed too, and managed to quiet the horse and hold on to his lance and even to move forward a little. His soldier's mind told him, 'There—in the throat—just below the jaw. Not the mouth, or he'll snap the lance.'

He waited and let the dragon come to him. He imagined he heard his old commanding officer say, 'Ah! that's how we do it in Rome!' and he grinned.

The dragon came on. And suddenly George gave a great yell—the yell a fighting-man gives to break his enemy's courage and to raise his own—and the monster closed its great, yawning mouth for an instant and lifted its head, exactly as George had hoped it would.

The lance slid into the soft, white flesh beneath the jaw—and held. And George held, and the horse held, too, though his hooves slithered on the muddy swamp-edge and twice he was fetlock-deep in water. The dragon rolled and thrashed about on the end of the lance and, failing to free itself, tried to drag horse and rider with it to their deaths. But that was a good Roman horse, he threw his weight back on his haunches and, with his front legs stiff and his hind-quarters almost on the ground, retreated step by agonizing step to the centre of the island.

Then, quite suddenly, it was over.

The people had been watching from the shore and now they came in boats to bring the hero home and to carry him, high on their shoulders, to the King whose only

daughter he had saved.

They were all dancing, singing, shouting his praises, pouring wine for him, kneeling at his feet, flinging chains of flowers about his neck. It was more than he could bear.

'It was nothing,' he said. 'A very little dragon, I could have led that small dragon on your princess' girdle...'

He was very weary.

'But there is something else I have to do,' he said. But what was it?

'Marry the princess,' they said. 'Marry the princess and be our King.' Certainly she looked very lovely with the white flowers in her hair, she reminded him of someone...

'No,' he said. 'She will marry someone else. I am quite sure of it.'

Then he remembered that he had promised to baptize them all, to make them the people of the God who had helped him to kill the dragon. And this he did, one after the other, beginning with the King, then the King's daughter, and then all the rest, ending with a tiny child less than three months old.

At last he went away on his own and slept.

He rode away next morning while the village still lay asleep. All the monster's venom had been washed away with its death, and where the marsh had been there was a blue lake again. Soon, he thought, there would be cattle and sheep in the fields, and new marriages would be made, and churches built. He wondered if the people would ever find themselves paying tribute to Rome.

George went back to Silene, reported to his superiors and took his punishment. Seeing that he was suffering from a desert-sickness, rambling about swamps and dragons and a girl with flowers in her hair, they were not hard on him, and the punishment was soon done. But his experience had evidently changed him in some way, and his fellow officers were not altogether sorry when he left the service and went away to settle in Diospolis in Palestine. A Christian, they thought, is never a comfortable companion—but a Christian who kills dragons in his sleep. . .

St. Mochae
and the Bird from Heaven

Of all the holy places in the world, Ireland is surely the holiest, with saints walking the length and breadth of it, from Malin Head to Youghal Bay, and from Dun Laoghaire to Ceann Leime in the west. There are many great stories written about St. Patrick and St. Brigid, and about Brendan the Voyager and about St. Columcille who was the friend of the angels of God—but there are other saints too, and some of them not well known at all.

There was Mochae the Beautiful who went to the Island of One Ridge on Loch Cuan, together with some other brothers who were looking for peace and unable to find it where there were men living. And surely there was peace on the island, as well as everything else they were needing—a fine big piece of country with trees on it, and grass for the few sheep and cows they had with them, and fresh water to drink when they were thirsty from the work.

It was a monastery they intended to build, but they put up a few small houses first, for themselves and the cows. That did not take long for all they wanted was a place to lie down in and a roof over their heads; there would be time enough later to think of building a great room where they could all eat together, and another where books might be written.

The cows settled themselves near the houses, and the sheep spread out across the island to find their own places, the way sheep like to do, and the brothers had as much peace as they wanted.

One day Mochae said, 'We should be building the church now, before we do anything else. It's well enough in the summer to be saying our prayers in the open air, but it will be different when there's rain in the sky and a cold wind blowing from the loch.'

The other brothers agreed, so they went together to cut branches, and Mochae went with them.

They did not all stay in one place, for that would have been to strip the same trees until they were bare, but three of them went one way and two of them went another, and Mochae the Beautiful went along by himself, dreaming of the fine church they would have before winter, and the brothers praising God in it.

'Perhaps we could build a tower at the side of it,' he thought. 'With a bell like the one St. Ita gave to Mochoemoc.'

All that morning he cut branches until he had a load of them stacked and tied ready for carrying. And then he sat down to rest a minute because cutting branches is tiring work to a man not used to it. So he rested and watched where the bees were going from flower to flower, and listened to the busy noise they were making. He could hear the sheep calling in the distance and an insect clicking its legs in the long grass, and a bird singing in a blackthorn tree.

After a while of this, when Mochae was beginning to think of picking up his load and taking it to the place where the church would be, the bird hopped out to the end of the bough and put his head on one side and said: 'That's hard work you've been doing, Clerk.'

'It is that,' said Mochae. 'But it's good work too, for the

branches will be used in building a church, and may God bless the trees that gave them.'

'And God bless the work,' said the bird, the way the country people say when they see a man cutting peat or thatching.

It was obvious the bird did not intend to fly off just then, so Mochae said, 'And who is it who is speaking to me?' for it's a poor, uncivil thing when two creatures are talking together and neither knowing the name of the other.

'I'm an angel of God,' said the bird, 'one of the people of heaven.'

'And I'm Mochae,' said the man, 'a monk of God living in the peace of this island. There are some others with me, and a few cows and sheep, and we're building a monastery down in the hollow.'

'I've seen it,' said the bird.

'Will you tell me about heaven,' said Mochae. 'For it's some time before I'll be seeing that, surely.'

'It's much the same as this place,' said the bird, looking around. 'A man would be hard pressed to choose between them.'

That pleased Mochae, for it is a good thing to know that the patch of earth you have chosen to live on is the same as the piece God has chosen for himself.

'But if that's the case,' he said, 'you're having little enough change in coming here.'

'That's the truth, indeed,' said the bird. 'But I came to speak the word of God to you, and to give you good cheer. Will you listen now, while I sing you three songs?'

'I will, and gladly,' said Mochae.

* * *

Then the bird from heaven sang three songs to Mochae the Beautiful, and in each of the songs there was fifty years.

And the leaves fell from the trees, and new buds opened all along the branches and their green darkened and turned to red and brown and gold and the leaves fell again. And bare boughs tossed in the wind, and birds came and built their nests and reared young ones, and flew away and there came others to take their place. And there were some trees that grew old and died, and there were others that were no more than a seed in the ground and they grew tall, with great, strong, spreading boughs on them, and men lying under them in the heat of the day.

And five times the course of the stream changed, running down from the hill, and green plants grew in the damp places all among the stones. And there was a drought that lasted a while until the stream was a trickle the width of a man's forearm and the beasts that drank from it had a sharp look, the way you could see their bones sticking up. And then the rain came. There was a flood, one time, and a wall built to hold the water back, and a night of storm when part of the wall fell in and the stream running through the gap like a torrent.

And Mochae stayed there, in the middle of the wood, listening to the songs during three times fifty years, and the time was like the passing of a single hour until the bird finished his singing.

Then Mochae picked up the load of branches he had cut and went to the place where he intended to build the church. But there was a church standing already, with a bell-tower at the side of it and a strange monk coming to pull the rope and set the bell swinging.

'What place is this?' asked Mochae, putting his load down.

'It's the church that was built to the memory of Mochae the Beautiful,' said the monk.

'What!' said Mochae. 'Don't you know who I am?'

'I do not,' said the monk. 'But you're very welcome.'

So Mochae went along with the monk, and he was sure there would be someone there who knew him and could say how the church was built so quickly, and himself in the woods for only a day.

But when they came to the hollow where the brothers had built shelters for themselves and the cows, there was a great stone house there with windows in it and there were more cows on the grass in front of the house than Mochae had ever seen in one place together. In the house thirty monks were sitting down to a meal of bread and cheese, and four or five others coming in at the door. While they ate, a monk was reading to them out of a great Gospel book with coloured pictures in the margin.

'For the love of God,' said Mochae, 'will you tell me what place this is, for I've never seen it before.'

'It's the monastery Mochae built in the old days,' they said. 'But it was only sticks then and poor, small houses like those they had for the cows. If he were to come back now, God rest him, he'd hardly know it.'

'Then what happened to him?' asked Mochae. 'Is he dead?'

And he gripped the edge of the table with both hands for fear of what they would tell him.

'There's no one alive can answer that,' they said. 'But not long after the brothers came to the Island of the One Ridge, they went into the wood together to cut branches for building a church. And Mochae did not come back. They looked for him in the wood from one end of it to the other, and across the island and away over the ridge. There were even two of them rowed out on the loch with nets to see whether the poor man was drowned—but not a trace of him did they find anywhere.'

'When did this happen?' said Mochae, knowing in his own mind that it was the same day he had gone out in the morning to cut branches for the church.

The monks thought about that and argued a bit among themselves, and then one said, 'It was a hundred and fifty years ago today.'

And Mochae whistled under his breath and said, 'Is it so?'

Then he told them how he had gone out that day and cut branches, and sat a while in the woods, listening to the bees, and how the bird from heaven had sung three songs to him.

'And there must have been fifty years in each of those songs,' he said. 'And myself no more than a day older.'

When they had all finished talking about the wonder of it, they took Mochae and showed him all the changes that had been made the while he'd been listening to the bird from heaven. There was a room where the brothers slept and another where they copied books, and another where the business of the monastery was done. There was a pond with fish in it, and there was a storehouse, and fine strong sheds for the cows.

Then they went back to the church with him and he showed them the branches he had cut one hundred and fifty years before that day, and the sap was still in them as though they were fresh-cut.

'Which they are,' said Mochae. 'A hundred and fifty years are nothing to God.'

They made a shrine with those branches because they were touched with the holiness that was on Mochae, and could not have been used for anything base. And they wrote the whole story in a book, just as Mochae told it, but the book has been lost since, destroyed by the heathen Norsemen.

But one other thing they did. They built a church in the middle of the wood, on the spot where the bird from heaven had sung the three marvellous songs to Mochae. And the walls of that church are standing today.

Queen Sunniva

Had it been given her to choose, Sunniva would have lived and died a nun and there might have been no story to tell, but as she was the only child of a king she had no choice. When her father was in his grave the people could not, or would not, govern themselves, so Sunniva left the peaceful grey walls of her convent and came into the world again, to give heart to them, as queens had always done in the old tales.

She was young, slender as a birch tree and as lovely as the green hills; the fame of her beauty and justice spread through the whole of Ireland and across the sea, and many fine men offered to marry her and share her fortune. Some of them were kings and had great names in the world, but she refused them all, saying the same thing to each, that she had not left the convent to marry any man—though he were as rich as the High King of Ulster, as invincible as Cuchullain himself, or as wise as all the wise men of Ireland thrown together. This was a refusal any man might take without shame—but there was a Viking chief who wanted her too, and for him a refusal, however worded, was something he could not accept.

'When my Vikings have killed her fighting-men and driven away her cattle and thrown a torch or two into her granaries, she may change her mind,' he said thoughtfully. 'In any event we will gain something.'

When Sunniva heard how her answer had been received, and that the Viking chief was provisioning his ships for war, she called her people together and said, 'It is because of me that this danger is coming to our land. If I stay here, there will be dishonour for us all.'

But the people answered, 'Let them come. We will fight them, Lady.' They looked fiercely towards the sea and clashed their spears against their shields to show their queen that they were not afraid, but in their hearts they knew they were too few to hold out for long.

Sunniva said, 'They will fire the corn, and drive away the cattle. If you manage to stay alive, you will live miserable, hunted lives—though I think it more likely that you will be killed. I say it were best that you go now to neighbour princes, and take your cattle with you, and whatever gold and weapons you have, that you may be received as men and not as slaves running before an enemy. When this sea-king comes, he will find an empty land—let him burn that if he will.'

'And what of you, Lady?'

'Why,' she said, taking the golden circlet from her head and laying it aside, 'I know a kingdom greater than any in this world, and a high King I trust above all men. I will throw myself upon his mercy and take what comes.'

She had expected to go alone, but when she went down to the harbour there were many of her people waiting, enough to fill three ships. They went on their knees to her and said they would go with her even to the edge of the world where the ocean falls in an endless cataract. Aye, and beyond that too if she willed it. It would have gladdened the heart of any queen to see them.

Sunniva said, 'It is not for me to say that we should go

here or there, but for God to direct us. We must leave our sails and rudders and oars behind us on the quay, and submit our lives to God's hand as the saints did long ago.'

Those were fearful words, but she meant them. One by one the masts were lifted from their cradles and laid on the stones, with the furled sails beside them, the oars stacked like wood for a beacon fire, and the rudders leaning against all.

'Your spears and shields too,' said Sunniva, and again she was obeyed, but silently, for it is a terrible thing to part a man from his weapons.

The three ships drifted out to the open sea, and the current took them and carried them north towards Scotland, where the waves beat against rocky islands and there was no sound but the roar of the ocean and the scream of gulls. Then the islands were behind them, and for days there was only the sea on every side. Sunniva's ship led, herself standing in the prow with her long rust-coloured hair streaming in the wind and seeming the only coloured thing in all that waste of grey water and white spray and the wreaths of black weed that floated and sank and rose again all round them.

Then, at last, a grey mountainous coast appeared on the horizon and loomed larger at every moment until it could no longer be mistaken for a mere bank of fog such as had fooled them more than once into thinking they were close to shore. Before long, strips of dark forest could be distinguished, and the tender green of cultivated land, and then a scattering of houses. Now they could smell pine trees and the smoke of fires.

Sunniva's old counsellor, who had been with her father, cried out in thankfulness. He had found the

voyage almost beyond endurance, holding that water was suited only to fish and scaly creatures, and not the proper element for men who had been born with legs to stand on.

'Wait,' said Sunniva, 'our voyage may not be over yet.' And the ships, drifting on, were greeted by a shower of stones and arrows.

'We should have brought our spears,' muttered one man, and the others agreed, but Sunniva frowned them to silence.

'They think that we are sea-raiders,' she said. 'And who can blame them?'

Again the current took them and carried them out of the range of bows and slings. A storm blew up, separating the ships and flinging them this way and that in the pounding dark. One was driven aground on Kinn, a small island north of Sognefjord, and some say that all in it were drowned, but others say they survived and remained on Kinn for many years, mourning their comrades.

But Sunniva's ship, and the other that went with her, drifted north and north again into a broad bay that had islands in it, and submerged rocks. Then they were turned aside by a steep, overhanging cliff that shone blue in the icy sunlight, and they could go no further. The tide spun them round and edged them, gently now, towards one of the islands and into a narrow creek between walls of red rock.

'Praise God,' said Sunniva, and clambered out to scale the cliff, with her people behind her, fearful that they had escaped a spear-death at home only to die of starvation on a rock.

Selje, where they had landed, was not so bleak a place

then as it is now. There was a grassy plain and an abundance of fresh water; there were trees and the tough wild plants that thrive in salt-laden air, and green moss clinging to the rocks. To the west a curving ridge dropped steeply to the sea and, on its summit, guillemots and razorbills laid their eggs, scorning to make nests such as the soft-living birds of the mainland build.

'We are not guillemots, Lady,' said one of Sunniva's people. 'Where shall *we* sleep this night, and other nights?'

That was answered easily. In the mountains there were caves, deep and dry and sheltered from the strongest wind that might blow from the sea.

'God provides all things,' said Sunniva. And that night her people lay warm on beds of fern and moss while she sat wakeful, watching the embers of her fire and thinking of all the days that were to come.

'Dear God,' she said. 'My people are your people, help me to keep them safe.'

And what was there on Selje that could harm them? It was a good life they had—not like their old life in Ireland with the rivers a-leap with silver salmon and the forests running with game, but good in its own way. They could not go hungry with the bountiful sea on every side. The men waded in the shallows with nets and the youths plundered the rocks for eggs; the women washed their clothes in cold spring water and mended them with fishbone needles; the children fetched branches and dead moss for kindling.

Sunniva, who had been a queen, ruled the island as though it were a convent, dividing each day into times for work, for leisure, for devotion. She taught her people to sing the Psalms she had learned among the nuns, she taught them to pray, and she made for them a chapel in the deepest cave, giving her own golden arm-bands to be beaten into a shallow chalice that they might celebrate the Eucharist together—though it was water they shared, not wine.

Selje was like a fortress and no man had ever seen fit to settle it. But there were other islands in the bay that were less difficult of access and these the mainland folk of Stadt and Moldefjord used as pasture for their cattle. When they looked across to Selje and saw it occupied, they feared for their beasts.

They said, 'No right man lives on a rock with birds for company. These people look to steal our cattle and bide their time.'

And they sent swift messengers to Haakon Jarl, a great lord in the north lands, saying that Vikings had made a lair on Selje and were filling their bellies with good Stadtland meat.

'It will be true by the time word reaches Haakon Jarl,' they said. 'Must we wait till a whole herd is lost before we act?'

Fear breeds fear and makes it hard to tell truth from falsehood. Many whose beasts were fattening on the low holmes in the bay, and calving too, were ready to swear that they had lost all to the raiders. Moreover, they believed it, as surely as if they had seen their cattle slaughtered. Axes were sharpened and beacons lit all along the coast, and men boasted that they would make blood-offering if the gods would give them victory.

Thus Haakon Jarl set out, armed for war, against the gentle Christians of Selje.

A boy gathering eggs among the high rocks saw the long ships coming and ran to warn Sunniva.

'I saw the sun glint strangely, Lady,' he said. 'I think there are weapons on those ships, and shields.'

'Then it is time to go into the chapel,' said Sunniva. 'Go, call the people together.'

They came up from the sea, and from the plain, from the rocks and springs, and they went into the chapel together, trusting Sunniva.

'I am not afraid to die,' said a woman with a child at her breast, 'so long as my soul is safe. But, Lady, who can promise me that?'

'Why, God has promised it,' said Sunniva.

'So I believe now, while my child is in my arms,' said the woman. 'My hand is in my husband's hand and we are together, one family. But if my husband should take a spear in his throat and leave me widowed, if I should see my child carried away and hear her screaming . . . surely I would curse God for ever, and then, Lady, what would become of my soul?'

Others spoke in the same way, agreeing that they were not afraid of death, whatever form that death should take, but that they feared to lose their trust in God.

They said, 'If we might all die now, praising God, we would be glad, knowing that we are safe through eternity, and together. Otherwise, who may answer for us or say what we shall do?'

'Do you trust God now?' Sunniva asked them. 'Do you abide strong in his will to save you, however he may choose to do it?'

They said, 'We do, Lady. And we are not afraid to die.'

Then Sunniva prayed that they might rest always in

God's will and that, whatever happened, their bodies, whether alive or dead, should not fall into the hands of the heathen.

And, in an instant, the roof of the cave fell in upon them, and a mass of rock sealed the openings of all the caves. It was a quick death, so quick that they did not know it; they died praying, parents and children together, their faith whole.

Haakon Jarl's men heard the loud thunder of falling rock and saw great stones bounce down the cliffs into the sea. They thought that the Selje people—they who had set the men of Stadtland trembling—were preparing to fight them off, and they grinned at each other, thinking of the sport they would have. But when they had scaled the red cliffs above the creek where Sunniva's ships had landed, they found no one. They searched the island from north to south, spreading out over the plain with their swords in their hands; they walked the mountain ridge, leaping across the new-made crevices, and they peered over the western drop into the empty sea. But there was no living soul on all the island.

'Those Stadtland men have had bad dreams,' they said. 'They are like drunken hen-wives who see foxes in every shadow.'

'It is from eating too grossly of their own meat,' said Haakon Jarl. 'The vapours from their bellies have risen into their heads...'

And, rowing back to the mainland, they made a song about the Stadtland Vikings, and lost their resentment in laughter.

But that is not the end of the story.

There came a time when Tord Eigleivsson and Tord Jorunnsson, two young men from south Firdafylke, set out to visit the Earl of Lade in Trondheim and, sailing northward along the coast, anchored off Selje for a night. The weather was fine and they were not inclined to sleep but sat talking together, boasting of their exploits as though they were old campaigners. And, as they talked, the sky lightened so that they thought dawn had come. Yet it was not dawn, for the light was coming from above and not from the horizon as is usual.

'It points to Selje,' said Eigleivsson.

'Aye—or from there,' said the other.

Many otherwise fearless men would have raised anchor at once and continued their voyage, thinking it best not to meddle with what is strange—but these two were young and feared nothing at all so they went briskly ashore to find the source of the light.

The brightness made a path across the plain to the foothills, but the mountain itself seemed as though it were all ablaze.

'In this way treasure-hoards are shown,' said Jorunnsson. 'We are in luck, brother.'

And they began to dig, loosening the stones with their knives, and scrabbling at the earth with their hands, working in haste lest the light should go out as suddenly as it had come. But it grew stronger until it seemed to focus sharply on one point and there they dug deeper.

It was not treasure they uncovered but a skull, snow-white and shining smooth, bright as a torch-flare and sweet-smelling as mown hay.

They did not speak, for it seemed to them that words would profane this place that some god had made sacred. It would be wise to leave before that god grew angry—both felt it so. And one of them took off his good linen shirt and wrapped the skull in it, for who would believe the tale they would later tell unless they had some proof with them?

Once safe away from Selje, they unwrapped the skull and looked at it again. Its light was dimmer now; it shone like pearl rather than like silver.

'We will take it to Haakon Jarl,' said Eigleivsson. 'He too has a tale of Selje, I remember, and perhaps he will know the meaning of this thing.'

Tord Jorunnsson began to sing the song of the Stadtland Vikings, which was well known in the north.

'Why, that was nothing,' he said. 'He was called out to war against an empty island. The Stadtlanders still blush for their part in it.'

'Aye—but perhaps the island was not so empty...'

Quickly they wrapped the skull again and stowed it away in a chest. Such matters were best not talked about at sea.

But when they reached the settlement of Haakon Jarl they found it desolate. An old man with his head bandaged came out of the forest and told them that the old ways were changing, Haakon Jarl was dead and his house broken.

'Olaf Tryggveson now rules in Norway,' he said. 'And it goes ill with Haakon's following.'

'If the times be changing, we had best change too,' said Jorunnsson. 'And since we have come so far, we might as well go further and see what manner of man King Olaf proves to be.'

'He's a Christian,' the old man said, and spat contemptuously.

* * *

King Olaf welcomed the voyagers and, as he seemed a fair-minded man as well as the strongest king in the north, they decided to hear what he had to say about this new faith of his, and whether it were likely to serve as well as the old. King Olaf spoke agreeably, offering his friendship and protection in return for their consent to be baptized, and they did not hesitate.

'If Haakon Jarl had listened as we have done, he would be alive today,' they said.

When the ceremony was over and they found themselves none the worse for it, they remembered the Selje skull and brought it out to show the King, who saw at once that it was a relic of great holiness. Bishop Sigurd, who sat at his right hand, said the same and he was so reluctant to part with it that Eigleivsson said he might keep it.

'It has brought us luck already,' he said, 'for now we have the friendship of a great King. It would be ungenerous of us to expect more from it.'

The next autumn King Olaf himself sailed south to Stadtland to find out what was known there concerning Selje. At first the people were disinclined to speak, for they had suffered enough mockery from their neighbours, but at last one old peasant admitted that he had been on the island one evening and had seen a light streaming from the mountain and spreading in a great fan across the sky.

'You may be sure I did not stay long,' he said. 'My fields on the mainland, and even my wife, seemed suddenly very dear to me.'

So King Olaf set out for Selje. It was fortunate that all

his oarsmen were Christian, for no other would have gone willingly with him. There was something wrong with the island—that much all men knew—and it is a foolish fellow indeed who goes against an enemy he cannot see.

The King and his followers went up the mountain, searching the scree as they went, and moving stones and great boulders aside. Here and there they found human bones, and these they gathered together, wrapping them in soft cloth and passing them back for the priests to guard.

And high up near the curving crest of the mountain they came to a place where a fallen slab of rock stood like a door, wedged tight against all their efforts to move it. King Olaf sent men back to the mainland for iron bars and, while he waited, the sea-birds—guillemots and skuas and petrels—came down from the heights to watch.

Even with the iron bars, and all men helping, it took some time to shift the rock. But at last it was done and King Olaf—with his hand on his sword and old tales of trolls and dragons springing to life in his mind—went into the cave. He need not have feared. There was nothing there but the body of a young woman, as slender as a birch tree and as lovely as the green hills. In her hands, half-hidden by her long, rust-red hair, she held a chalice of gold, roughly made but with a cross scratched on it.

'She sleeps,' said Olaf Tryggveson, but when he touched her cheek with one finger, he knew that she was dead.

King Olaf built a church in the rock at the cave of St.

Sunniva, and shrines were made to house the bones of the Selje people. The saint herself lay in King Olaf's church for many years until 1170 when her shrine was removed to Bergen.

The Flying Walking-Stick

The legends of the saints are rich in signs and wonders. There are stories of thorns that flower in midwinter and of statues that weep real tears; there are moving stories of the sick made well at a touch, and there are homely tales like this one of St. John-Joseph of the Cross.

In his youth, when he had first become a monk, John-Joseph had carried stone for the builders of his monastery at Piedmonte di Alife in Italy and had never troubled himself about the weather. People said that he had gone barefoot in the snow and carried weights beyond his strength, and so he may have done but he could not remember clearly. He had been old and lame now for many years, and his limbs were good only for telling him when there was rain in the air. His stout stick was more useful to him than his legs were.

He smiled at the things people said. When he had last visited Ischia, his birth-place, they had hailed him as a saint and jostled each other for the privilege of touching his hand. They said his touch healed them—yet he had not been able to heal himself when the illness had robbed him of his senses and left him numb along one side and trembling on the other.

'Only God heals,' he said.

People spoke of other miracles too, claiming that he had many times divided a few crusts between more than a score of men in such a way that each received a whole loaf as his share. And he shook his head, saying, 'But only God is able to satisfy hunger.' Surely people were very foolish to read miracles into such simple things. He had done only what there was to do, and no man can do more than that.

Now he was too old to do much. He had been born on the Feast of the Assumption in the year 1674—which meant that he must be approaching eighty. That was a fine age for such a frail old fellow to reach and, thank God, he could still go about the streets of Naples and hear the news of the day; he could still bless the new-born babies, and mourn with widows and pray by the candle-lit biers of the dead. Awkward and ungainly he might be, leaning on his stick, hopping and flapping along like an old bald-headed crow, but at least he was not confined to his bed yet. He could still enjoy the unlimited variety of Naples, the light and shade, richness and squalor, the lovely sweep of the bay, and above all, the people.

And he could still get to the cathedral and praise God for the ever-recurring miracle of St. Januarius' blood. The cathedral was surely blessed in possessing such a holy relic—a phial of dull, reddish dust that not only on the saint's own Feast-day, but eighteen times a year, showed itself as though newly shed, a rich and liquid ruby, the life-stream of a martyred bishop. John-Joseph, although he had witnessed this miracle more than a hundred times, could still be moved to tears by it.

There were hard-headed men in those days, as there are now, who would say that it was nothing but trickery, or perhaps produce some scientific explanation—but John-Joseph was himself too honest to look for trickery in others, and too devout to see science as a rival to faith. He was content to accept what he saw, to believe that his eyes saw truly, and to marvel at the benevolence that allowed such things to be.

'If blood is life,' he said, 'here is sure proof of the eternal life to come. God demonstrates it to us in this way because, in his pity for us, he knows that we cannot understand what we do not see.'

One morning, on the Feast of St. Januarius, he rose early so that he might be at the cathedral in good time before the crowds gathered. But one thing after another delayed him—a bird singing on a branch outside his narrow window, a tangle in his beard, a mislaid sandal. And he was interrupted a dozen times, it seemed, by unexpected visitors who meant to say no more than 'Good morning' and 'God bless you', but who stayed a while to reminisce, as old men do.

So it was later than usual when John-Joseph set out, and by the time he reached the cathedral he was breathless and a little flustered at finding so many there before him, such a press and pushing of bodies—ladies in their wide, whalebone-stiffened skirts and gentlemen as fine as birds of paradise; clerks and apprentices making the most of their holiday; merchants and their wives; fruit-sellers, fishermen, gardeners and labourers; thieves and pickpockets and tousle-haired, sluttish girls with painted faces and torn petticoats.

John-Joseph hesitated in the doorway and wondered what he should do. It would not be easy to find a place for himself in so huge a crowd, and it would not be proper to expect anyone to move aside for him. But, after all, the decision was not his to make. He was pushed forward from behind as more and more latecomers arrived, he was carried along on their volition and not his own—forced between hips and shoulders and jutting elbows into spaces too small to contain even his slight frame, and then pushed on again, struggling to keep his balance though often his head seemed so far in advance of his feet that he would have fallen had there been room enough to fall in.

Then he lost his stick.

It was knocked from his hand at a moment when the crowd surged forward. A young labourer saw it fall and tried to retrieve it but too late, the space was filled at once and the stick lost underfoot.

'Well, it is not too bad,' thought John-Joseph. 'At least I am held upright by the people.' And he allowed himself to be carried along as before.

He saw the precious phial raised in the white hands of the priest, and heard the people gasp with a wonder that never staled; his own eyes filled with tears.

And somehow he found himself back at the cathedral door, brought there, he supposed, on the returning wave of those who had seen and were now dispersing. And there he remained like a piece of driftwood left by the tide, for he could go nowhere without his stick. He could not even stand.

That being so, he must sit. The day would not be longer than other days and sooner or later the cathedral would empty and his stick be found. Meanwhile he had the sun to enjoy, and the carriages to watch, and the children to recite their catechism to him.

The hours passed, the sun rose higher in the sky and seemed to hang there, burning. The shadows were sharp as knives. People came and went, came and went, and still John-Joseph sat, exchanging greetings and praising God for so much devotion shown to St. Januarius.

Now the aristocracy arrived to see the miracle. With their powdered wigs and the tiny velvet patches on their cheeks, they looked like creatures from a different world. The ladies wore veils over their crimped and curling hair, but their arms were bare from elbow to wrist. They walked as modestly as nuns, but their slippers had bold red heels such as no nun ever wore. And the lords did not look devout at all, they carried their hats in their crook'd arms and bowed to all their acquaintance with a great flourishing of scented handkerchiefs.

'They are like pretty, frivolous children,' thought John-Joseph, 'dressed up to rival the flowers because it is a holiday. It is vanity, but what does it matter? They go to honour the saint.'

Then came the noble Duke of Lauriano in his family coach that was cushioned in yellow silk and drawn by two proud horses the colour of burnished copper.

He saw John-Joseph sitting there with his trembling old hands clasped about his knees, and his head nodding.

He said, 'Why, Father, what is the matter with you, sitting there like the ancestor of all beggars, when you should be at home, resting in the shade?'

John-Joseph said, 'I have good reason, son. I have lost my steed and how may an old man, with his legs already in the grave, get home unaided?'

Pride is for people uncertain of their station, and the Duke of Lauriano was no prouder than a peasant.

He said, 'Ride with me, Father. I will see you home before I attend at the cathedral. Come.'

But John-Joseph shook his head.

'That is kind of you, my son. But how may I leave without my own steed, that serves me faithfully? My walking-stick,' he explained, 'that has carried me for more years than I well remember, lies inside.'

The Duke laughed and said, 'That is easily put right, Father. I will play the groom's part and fetch your steed myself.'

And he went into the cathedral.

But John-Joseph's steed was no longer waiting to be fetched.

All the people congregated in the nave were gazing upwards and crying, 'A miracle! *Another* miracle!' and the knobbed old staff came flying through the air above their upturned faces. It flew no higher than two hands'-breadths above the tallest head, yet no one reached up to stay its flight. Those on the outer edges of the crowd could not see clearly what was happening, but they felt the disturbance flowing out to them from its centre and called out, 'What is it? What is it?'

Some thought the cathedral must be toppling, and others that fire had broken out, while one old woman, almost blind, insisted shrilly that Christ was come again.

On the stick flew, not fast but steadily. The Duke of Lauriano, standing near the door, saw the stick pause in the air as it reached the threshold, as though bewildered by the sunlight.

Is *this* a miracle, he wondered, an old stick hacked from a branch, God knows how many years ago, dead wood flying direct as a feathered arrow to its master's hand? A miracle? No, it was too absurd, too comical. And yet...

The stick flew straight towards John-Joseph where he sat on the steps. It struck him lightly on the breast and

dropped into his hand.

'Ah, there you are,' said John-Joseph, and gripped it firmly. 'We must take care not to lose each other again.' And he hobbled off as briskly as he was able.

The people ran from the cathedral, racing and tumbling down the steps to see what would happen next. But there was nothing to see, only an old man they all knew and dearly loved, limping away down the street with his stick in his hand, exactly as they had seen him a thousand times before.

The old blind woman whimpered at the Duke's elbow, 'Where is he? Let the Lord give me back my sight.' And the Duke sighed and said, 'No, old woman. It is not the Lord this time—but it would seem we have another saint in our midst.'

William Firmatus and the Savage Boar

It was a fine spring morning when young William Firmatus rode out from the city of Tours to serve his lord. His mind was full of great and glorious thoughts, but a corner of it was set aside for himself. He had vowed his sword-arm to whatever cause his lord might consider just—but he also intended to get what he could of the spoils of battle for, he reasoned, even a soldier must pay his way in the world and put aside something for the future.

He was a widow's only son and she was proud of him. For years she had walked the knife-edge between indulgence and strictness, falling now on one side and now on the other; she had been offered more advice than she could use, and far more than she was willing to take. Her brothers had said, 'Put him to the law, sister, or to a trade. Then when he is older, he will care for you.' And the priest had said, 'No, mistress, give him to the Church. A widow's house is no place for a headstrong boy.'

She had listened first to one side, then to the other, seeming to weigh what was said to her. But she always replied, 'Let him choose for himself. I shall be satisfied if he grows to be such a man as his father was. Whatever he does, he will care for me in my old age, and he will always give the Church its due.'

So, alternately, William had run wild and kept close to

his books, and, now that he was a man, had chosen to be a soldier.

Yet, within five years, he was home again. He had gained a few scars and a saddlebag full of gold coins. He had also seen men die.

'It is better to save life than to take it, mother,' he said. She kissed his forehead, though he had to stoop to her now, he had grown so tall.

'Whatever you choose to do will be right,' she said. And, though his uncles snorted their displeasure and the priest shook his head, William set himself to the study and practice of medicine.

He had aptitude and did well. He wore a robe as rich as a merchant's and the silver dishes he gave his mother were as fine and costly as any in a lady's house. He gave to the Church from his surplus, and he remembered the poor—when it did not pinch him too hard to do so.

His mother praised him, and his uncles were satisfied, but the priest saw something in the depths of his eyes and said, 'I reserve my judgement. There is more to William than a scalpel and a book of cures.'

William gained in riches and reputation. But he gave away less, and saved more.

'I must be prudent,' he said. 'I must think of tomorrow. All the same, you may be sure I refuse no man who is worthy of help.'

The priest sipped the wine William poured for him and thought, this is not the best in his cellar. He said, 'What man *is* worthy? If you can tell me that, you are wise indeed.'

'I live in the world,' said William. 'And I may say that I know a little of men.' And he wondered how so fat a priest dared hint that he was too close with what was, after all, his own.

His great chest of money stood at the foot of his bed, where it would be safe from robbers. 'I do not care so very much for gold,' he told himself. 'But what I have earned, I will keep.'

And he slept well.

'The night it disturbs my sleep, I will know I am a miser,' he said, and laughed.

But he slept less well.

'Only if I rise in the night to assure myself that it is there, will it have power over me,' he said.

And now he lay awake, listening to every creaking sound in the dark.

Then there came a night when he heard not only the familiar creaking but another sound—a chuckle. And it came from the end of the bed where the chest stood. At once William sat bolt upright and reached for his tinder-box and candle...

It was not a thief who was in the room—but something worse. Sitting on the great, carved chest, like an emperor on his throne, with William's fur-lined robe draped across its back, was a monstrous ape. It twitched at the fine woollen folds, and scratched its hairy chest, and chuckled again. And all the time its tiny red eyes watched William.

The candle shook in William's hand so that the flame soared and smoked. Hot wax dripped on his skin, but he did not feel it. He said, 'There is no ape in the room.'

Yet there it sat, scratching and chuckling. And William remembered what he had said, '... only if I rise in the night...' and he knew then that the ape was the Devil himself, and that gold had a terrible power.

'It shall not have power over me,' he said, firmly. The ape showed its yellow teeth and chattered.

'It shall not,' he said again, and crossed himself. The ape snarled and shrank back a little but was as real as ever, and William was ashamed that he had thought to use the cross as a talisman.

'More than that is required of me,' he said. And he climbed out of his great warm bed and went to the window; he passed his treasure-chest without a sideways look, and knelt down on the cold, stone floor with his back to the Devil, and prayed as he had never prayed before, not for the safety of his gold but that he might be delivered from the snare of avarice.

When morning came, he was haggard and shivering—but the Devil had fled and he was free.

'Now I must send for the priest,' he said, and then changed his mind. 'No, I will go to him myself.'

The priest sat by a blazing fire; he leaned back in his cushioned chair and listened to William's story.

'Give your money to the Church,' he said. 'And thank God every day, on your knees, that you have had such an escape.'

'No,' said William. 'I am willing to thank God every day that I live. But I will give my money to the poor. . .'

'The poor are everywhere,' said the priest, 'and you have but one fortune to give.'

'Then let the Church distribute it for me,' said William. 'But in bread, priest, not candles. And do not let my mother starve, for she too will be poor now that I go to serve God.'

For the second time in his life, William Firmatus left the city of Tours, but this time he went on foot with a staff in his hand, and was resolved not to get but to give. In country that had been ravaged by war, looted by soldiers such as he had been in his younger days, he used his skill in medicine to heal, and he took no payment other than food. He joined a band of pilgrims and travelled as far as the Holy Land, then turned about and came to France again. He passed through Tours and received his mother's blessing, but would not stay because here the poor treated him like a saint, kissing the hem of his ragged cloak, and his uncles treated him like a beggar, giving him bread at their doors.

'I am neither a saint nor a beggar,' he said. 'Merely a man who seeks God in all that lives...'

Then he went north and west until he came to Brittany, and there he settled, building a hut for himself on the edge of a forest. He was happy there; the country people accepted him as a good man, not as a saint. He cured them when they were sick and they fed him when he was hungry. And what food he had, he shared with the birds and beasts; even the foxes came, licking their grinning mouths, and he chided them for their greed as though they were children.

All lived together in harmony—except for one old boar who cared nothing for brotherly love. He and the villagers had been enemies for years, for he foraged as he chose, breaking down fences and spoiling what he did not eat. They had set traps for him, which he avoided; they had dug pits for him and he had scrambled out; they had hunted him and he had escaped.

'He's the Devil himself,' the people told William, showing him their trampled gardens. But William disagreed. *He* knew what the Devil was. The boar, he said, was no more than a thoughtless creature, ill-tempered and obstinate perhaps, but not beyond redemption.

'I will reason with him,' said William. 'No, not with a spear in my hand. We should reach no understanding that way.'

He went deep into the forest, where the tangle of undergrowth was thick and the branches of trees met overhead. It is as beautiful as a church, he thought, and more beautiful, because here the very pillars are alive and growing. No beast, living here, could be wholly bad.

In the deep, dark heart of the forest the old boar lifted his head and listened. He sensed the presence of Man in his territory—and Man was his ancient enemy.

Feeling the itch of old wounds, he rubbed his spear-scarred sides against a tree; he furrowed the beech-mast with his tusks; he snorted his rage, and stamped and listened again. Then swiftly, lightly, he began to run towards the sound. He would show this enemy, this man, who was lord of the forest.

He and William met in a glade, each coming out of the sheltering trees to meet the other—and each was determined on having his own way. Yet there was one difference between them. The boar was filled with anger, wanting only to kill—and William was filled with love, wanting only to save.

This was something the boar had never encountered. He knew how to knock the spear from a man's hand, leaving him helpless—but this man had no spear. He knew how to make use of a man's fear, and how to use a man's strength against himself. But this man had no fear and was as frail as a wind-tossed twig. The beast was puzzled.

So they faced each other. The boar stood still; he

would not charge before he had got the measure of this strange enemy. A man who goes into a forest with no spear and no strength and no fear must have a very potent weapon. It were better to wait and see what that weapon might be.

William moved forward, as though to greet an old acquaintance. The boar put down his head, but he was still uncertain and did not charge.

'You must make an account of yourself,' said William. 'For I have heard sorry tales about you. Indeed, with my own eyes I have seen evidence of your bad behaviour...'

Now they were very close and William could see the scars on the boar's shoulders and flanks where he had been wounded, not once but many times. He put out his hand and touched the scars.

'Are these your excuse?' he asked. 'Yet how can that be? Those whose gardens you have ruined, whose labour you have set at nothing, are not those who have harmed you, friend.'

The boar trembled at his touch, and backed away. But William took him firmly by the ear.

'And even if these simple folk *had* harmed you, brother, what use is it to harm them in return? There is enough evil in the world, and enough waste and sorrow, without adding more.'

The boar tossed his head and grunted, but William's grip was not to be shifted.

'You must repent,' he said, 'or some day the Devil will sit in your lair as he sat in my own room long ago. And you cannot go against the Devil with tusks, or crush him against a tree the way you would crush a man. No, my poor beast, you must repent and pray.'

As he spoke, he led the boar away through the forest

towards the village. The trees thinned, and the golden evening light glanced through their leaves. Together beast and man came into the open.

The village people talked of that day for many years. It was an event, something rare and marvellous, to be handed on to the next generation and the next, like a carved linen-press, or a warm cloak, or land—it was their own small miracle.

'... he came out of the trees, all golden like one of the blessed saints in a painted window, and the old boar at his side, gentle as a nursling lamb. But he was stern, mind you, he'd a will of his own, that man. He took the beast right up to his hut and he shut 'un in, saying, "You bide there and pray for forgiveness, and I'll stay here at the door and pray with you."

'And there he stayed all night, on his knees, like he were wrestling the Devil for the soul of that girt pig. And in the morning he let the creature out—all quiet and chastened he was—and sent 'un back to the forest...'

What more is there to tell? The boar truly repented of his sins and, though once in a while he came out of the forest to visit the man who had called him 'friend' and 'brother', he never again despoiled the village gardens. The villagers even put out food for him, turnips and greenstuff and apples that were only a little bruised; they would have defended their boar against the King's huntsmen if it had ever come to that.

William grew old, as thin as a dead leaf. For a long time he could not walk far without great effort. And one day he died, but he is still remembered as the saint who cared for the poor and humble, and for the beasts who could not plead for themselves.

St. Senan

There is a story told about Senan, that he spoke aloud when he was only seven days in the world, a wisp of a creature with his fingers and toes curled like the fronds of young ferns, and his head as wise as a mitred bishop's. His mother had gone to the spring to draw water, carrying him with her in a sling on her back. It was a good step from the house, the pitcher was heavy with the water in it, and the blackberries in the bushes along the path ripe and ready for picking, so Senan's mother thought she would eat one or two of them, just to refresh herself a little for the walk. It is not an easy thing, surely, to eat only a handful of fruit and leave the rest. She ate one or two of the berries and walked on, but then she stopped again and had a few more, and when she stopped for the third time she stayed for a long while, picking the berries from the top of the bush and working her way down till there were precious few left on that side of it for the birds, and her mouth and fingers were all stained with the juice.

But Senan called out, 'Is this the time to be eating and dreaming, with my father's dinner not cooked, and him waiting? Let the berries stay on the stalks, mother, and come back for them another time.'

This was a fine and unusual start to his life, but he did not say anything more for a year or two, till he was ready for it in the normal run of things, and there was nothing odd about what he said then.

He grew up to be a sensible, hard-working boy, a great help to his parents both in the house and outside it. They had two farms and lived sometimes in one and sometimes in the other, according to the season, and Senan would go ahead, when they moved, to get everything ready for them. He always had a comfortable house waiting, with the yard swept, and a fire burning and peat stacked near the door. And if anything needed mending, he would see to that too. His parents never had to come into a house that had the roof leaking or the door loose on its hinges.

But one day he forgot what was expected of him. He started off when he was told, but stopped on his way to look at a neighbour's pigs which were not thriving as well as they should. Then he stayed talking a while and was given a bite to eat and then, when he left the house, not thinking what he was doing, he went back to the place he had come from. His mother saw him coming in at the door when he should have been far away and, being worried with the business of getting the hens together and tying them down in the cart, she lost her temper with Senan.

'And what are you doing back here?' she demanded. 'Have you no thought for the state the house will be in, with the fire out and maybe a nest in the chimney for us to shake down in the dark? It's small use you are, Senan!'

There was no time to stand arguing, so they set off. And they had not gone very far before they saw all the farm-tools, and the household stuff, the pots and brooms and all the things Senan used to take with him, whirling through the air above their heads and with a purposeful look about them.

And when they got to the house the next day everything was in its right place, with the fire lit and a stew simmering, the way it had always been for their coming.

When a few more years had passed and Senan was grown to a fine tall lad, there came a day when his father decided the boy was old enough now to be responsible for the cattle. He and his wife would go ahead to the summer farm and this time Senan would follow after them with the beasts.

It was not an easy road—part of it ran along the edge of the shore and the cattle went so slowly that Senan was afraid the tide would be up before he had them more than half-way across. It would be better to wait till morning for that stretch of the journey, he thought, but if he did that he would have to find a place where he could keep them all together during the night and not wandering about in every direction.

There was a fortress nearby, owned by a man called Machar, who was very important in that country, and Senan thought he would ask Machar to lend him the use of his courtyard. It was a small thing to ask of a man with a great house like that one—but Machar was away from the fort at the time, and his steward was a twisty-eyed, arrogant man enjoying the power he had while it lasted, and he ordered Senan to be off. He slammed the door in his face, too.

That made Senan angry, but anger was useless to find a night's lodging for the cattle. He had no choice but to set off with them along the shore, with the dark coming down and the tide washing their heels.

When they were all safe above the line of high-water,

he looked back and saw how the sea was curling and foaming along the track they had followed, and he thanked God for the anger that had driven him and the beasts so fast.

He did not know until later that, in the night, robbers had broken into Machar's fort and plundered and burned it. When he heard that, it seemed to him that God had saved his life twice over—once from the robbers and once from the sea.

'It would be ungrateful of me to get on with my life as though nothing had happened,' he said. 'I'll leave the farm now and become a priest.'

Senan left the cattle with his father and went away to live with a holy man called Cassidan, who taught him the Psalms and the Gospels. But if Senan thought he had finished with farm work he was mistaken, for every youth learning priesthood from Cassidan had to take his turn at driving the cows and calves that belonged to the church out to their pasture. The other boys managed it well enough and never had the smallest bit of trouble, but when it came to Senan's turn the beasts had the devil in them. The cows had to be put in one field and the calves in another, but as soon as Senan had collected the calves together and got them where they belonged, the cows would follow them until each one was with her own calf again—and if he put the cows in their field first, then the calves would push themselves under the gate till every one of them had found its mother.

In the end Senan found a way round this. He drew a line with his stick between the cows and the calves, while the young ones were still trying to get under the gate.

'And don't let ever a one of you cross this line,' he said.

And, indeed, not one of them did all the time that Senan sat between them, reading the Psalms aloud from a book.

Every night, when all the cows had been milked and shut up in their stalls, Senan had to go to the mill that was in the monastery and grind corn for the next day's bread, and one night he asked the cook for a new candle because there were none left at the mill.

'I've only one left,' said the cook, 'and the new wicks have not yet been dipped in the tallow. But you're welcome to this one—at least it will see you through the night.'

He thought Senan would be back next day for one of the new candles, but he was not. And the cook never gave the matter another thought until the end of the week, and then he went to the mill himself to see how Senan was managing all this time in the dark. But there was a light coming out of the window that was like twenty candles burning and, when the cook looked in, there was Senan sitting reading while the mill ground the corn without any help from anyone.

The cook was surprised and a bit frightened, too, but he thought he might have imagined it, so he said nothing. He watched the next night, and again the night after, and it was exactly the same. The mill ground corn as though it had never needed a man's help with the work, and Senan sat reading in the light, turning page after page.

After that night, Senan's corn was all ground and it was time for one of the other lads to be grinding his. Senan took the candle back to the cook and thanked him—and the length of the candle was exactly the same after the tenth night as it had been on the first.

* * *

By this time Senan's fame had spread right through the country and there were a lot of people came to see him on one pretext or another. It seemed that everyone in Ireland wanted Senan to go and live with him and every single one of them had some special inducement to offer.

'Listen to what they all have to say, and choose for yourself,' said Cassidan. 'It's time you saw a bit more of the world.'

So Senan left Cassidan and went to live with the people of Inniscorthy for a while, because they were humble and that pleased him, and then he left there and went up and down the country, founding churches.

There was a time when he was staying with Bishop Setna on Innis Mor, where all the water that was used in the church was drawn from a holy well in the rock nearby. One day, when they were talking together, a crowd of monks came and complained that a woman had defiled the holy water by washing her child's clothes in the well. And surely, they said, it would not be proper now to use such water in the church.

The Bishop was a man of great book-learning. He knew as much Latin as the Pope did, but he had his own hard opinion of what was right.

He said, 'Indeed it is an evil thing, and only evil will come of it.'

'That was not well spoken,' said Senan. And almost at once another monk came running, to say that the woman's son was gone from her. The child had been playing at the edge of the cliff, where he had been told more than a score of times *not* to play, and his foot had slipped so that he had fallen over the edge into the sea.

Senan said to the Bishop, 'That was a bad thing you said, Bishop Setna, it was as if you were ill-wishing the child. Will you go out and find him now, and bring him to me, while I say a morsel of prayer for you both.'

Bishop Setna was ashamed, for he was not a wicked man, only lacking in grace. He was sorry in his heart that he had taken such a stubborn view of what the woman had done, for surely the holiness of a well was not of greater worth than the life of a little child. So he went out in a boat and rowed up and down beneath the tall cliffs, searching the water for a glimpse of the small body floating, and hearing in his mind the way the women would keen when he brought it home to them. And then his heart gave a great leap in his chest, enough to stop him breathing for a moment, for there was the child sitting astride the waves and laughing, and gathering up the foam in his hands as though it were flowers. The Bishop thanked God for his mercy and lifted the child into the boat and brought him to Senan, who gave him back to his mother, with as much life in him as he had ever had, and just as likely to play again on the edge of the cliff.

Then one of the monks, whose name was Libern, said: 'Even so, Senan, the well has been defiled, so that every woman in the place may wash her clothes in it and it will be none the worse, and what water shall we use for the church now?'

And Senan said, 'That's a fine crozier you have in your hand, and why should it not search out water for you? Remember Moses, Libern, and thrust the end of it into the earth, and see what will happen.'

Libern did that, because he had great faith in Senan after the woman's son was found alive again, and the water gushed out at his feet, and has never failed since. It is called the well of Libern to this day.

* * *

After that Senan left Innis Mor and went to live on the mainland, but he stayed near the edge of the sea because he liked to watch the waves racing along the shore, and hear the great fuss and bother the sea-birds made when the fishing boats came in.

He was sitting on a rock one afternoon, thinking what a fine day it was with the sun making a path across the sea and the gulls floating in and out of it, looking like jet one minute and like gold the next, when a stranger came up behind him.

'The peace of the day to you, Senan,' said the stranger. And Senan looked up and knew that it was the Archangel Raphael speaking.

'And the peace of the day to you,' he answered.

'Do you see that island out there in the middle of the sea?' said the Archangel. And Senan screwed up his eyes against the sun's glare, and said, 'I do.'

'There's a terrible monster lives on that island,' said the Archangel, 'and there's not a sinner can set foot in the place because of him. But if you were to go out there and found a church, he'd be cast out of it.'

'He would that,' said Senan.

'Will you go now?' said the Archangel. And Senan said there was no point in thinking it over, he would never be readier than he was at that moment.

So the Archangel lifted the rock with Senan sitting on it, and carried it across the sea.

The monster was stretched out almost the whole length of the island. Its body was covered with green scales and its head was something like that of a horse, with a long tangled mane hanging down its neck and over its face so that only one of its great red eyes could be seen, and its red nostrils snorting smoke and flames.

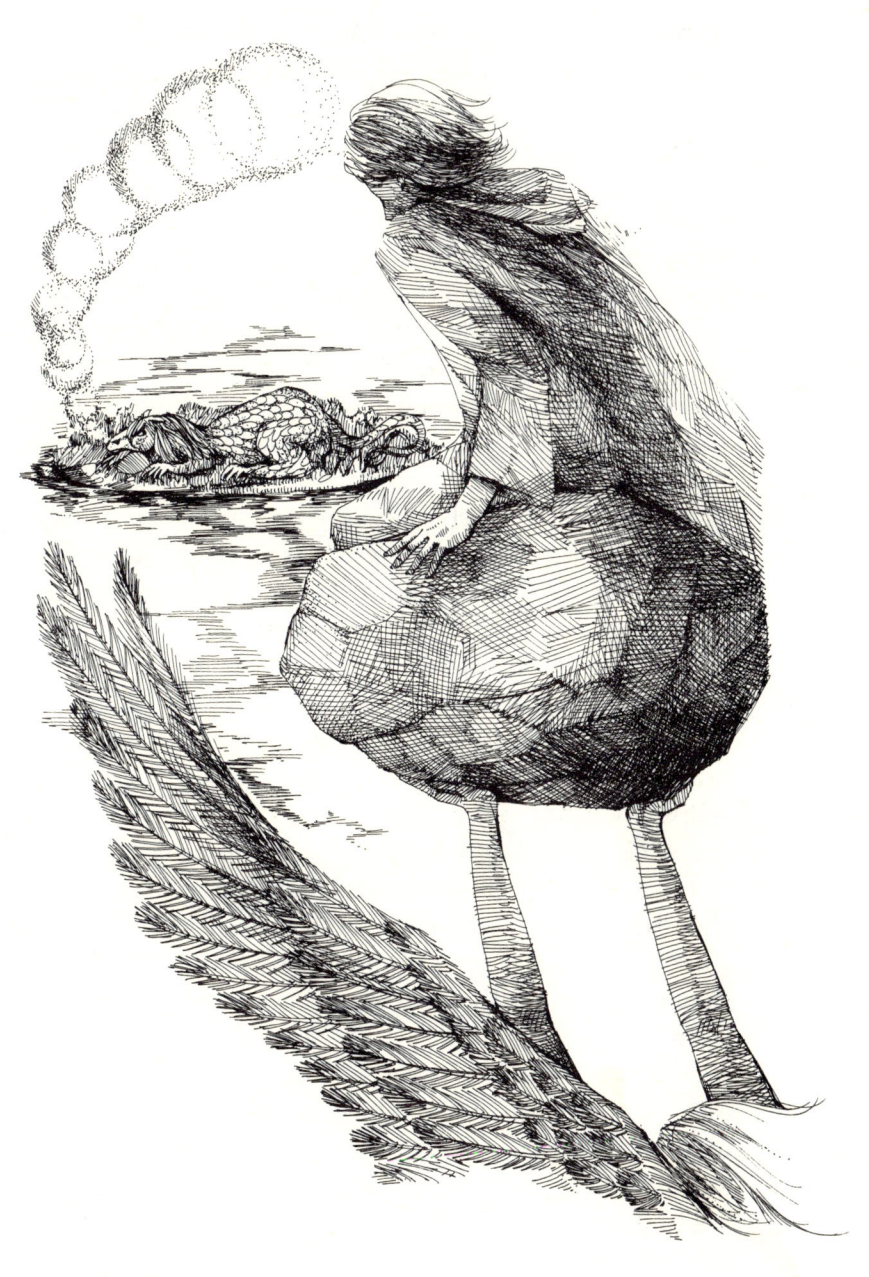

When it saw Senan it stood up to meet him, and there were iron claws on its feet that struck fire from the rocks as it moved over them, yard after scaly yard of it.

But Senan was not afraid. He reasoned that the Archangel Raphael would not have brought him to the place if any harm was likely to come of it, so he stayed where he was and let the creature come right up to him till he could feel his skin parched from the heat of its breath. Then he made the sign of the cross and said: 'I'm taking this island to build a church on it, so it's time you were away from here. I'll not be too hard on you, though. You can go anywhere you like in the world so long as you harm no one.'

And the monster shrank away into itself when it saw the cross, and the fire went out of it. Then it stepped down into the sea and swam over to the mainland, the way it was told, and from that day it harmed no one.

Now the King, who owned that part of the country where the island was, had no particular love for Christians. When he heard that Senan had settled down on the island he flew into a bellowing rage and sent two of his chieftains to drive the saint away. These two were called Coel and Liath and they were known as bad men to quarrel with, but Senan was no more afraid of them than he had been afraid of the monster. He looked at them quite calmly and said he was not going anywhere, they might point their spears at him as much as they liked.

'We can make you,' they said, and they took hold of him and started dragging him along the ground towards their boat. But after they had gone a little distance, Liath thought better of it and dropped the hand that he was holding.

'He's only a slip of a man,' he said, 'and he's doing no harm here. I'd rather have nothing to do with the matter.'

Coel said, 'The King has ordered us to do it. If we refuse, he will take our own lands from us, and our lives too if the mood is on him.'

Liath said, 'It would be easier for me to leave Ireland than to do wrong to Senan.'

There was nothing the other one could do if Liath stood against him, and though he cursed so that the angels would have wept to hear him, and though he threatened both Liath and Senan with every sort of ill that it is possible for one man to do to another, he had to admit himself beaten and row back to the mainland.

'You will not be so calm when I come back,' he said.

But Coel never did go back there, for as he went through the door of his house, his foot slipped and he fell, striking his head against a corner. And after that he was able to sit in his chair and have his food brought him, but he was no good for anything else.

The King's steward ran to his master to tell him all that had happened, that the saint had refused to leave the island and that Liath had upheld him.

'And Coel, who yesterday was a great, strong man and a match for any three others, sits on his chair today, as weak as a baby, while his wife spoons porridge into his mouth. There's not a man in your country who'll go out against the saint, because of that.'

'Men are fools,' said the King, and he sent for his bard. In those days a bard was not simply a man who could play on the harp and sing. He could string words together that would shrivel a man's heart in his body, or cause a horse to stumble, or raise a wind, or bring black mildew on the crops.

'I'll soon have him out of the island for you,' said the bard. 'But I'll want a reward.'

'You shall have it,' said the King. 'I'll give you the island itself.'

The bard considered that a fair reward for a job he would enjoy doing, and had himself rowed out to the island at once.

He stood there on the shore, chanting spells against Senan, and although it was the springtime of the year, all the young leaves on the trees curled up, and the green went out of them, as though winter were coming.

But Senan cared nothing at all for those words.

'That's nothing but empty sound,' he said. 'It's like a man clattering nutshells together.'

So the bard raised his voice a bit, and threw a spell into the sun's face so that the world was darkened.

Senan said, 'That's a poor small piece of a conjuring trick any boy can learn if he sets his mind to it.' And he put up his hand towards the sun and pulled the darkness down between his fingers, like a housewife pulling a cobweb down from the ceiling.

Then the bard called up a storm, with thunder and lightning, and a wind blowing the trees right down to the earth. There was sharp rain in the wind that stung Senan's face, and soaked through his clothes until he was wet to the skin, and freezing.

But the saint did not care about that either.

He made the sign of the cross into the storm, and the thunder died away. The wind and the rain stopped and the trees stood upright again and shook the water off their branches, the way a dog does, coming out of the river.

So the bard had the worst of that too, and he had to

admit it, and Senan stayed on the island and finished building his church.

He was an old man by that time and felt he had founded enough churches in Ireland to have earned a rest from the work. So he decided to remain where he was—he would not be lonely at all, for some monks had come from the mainland and built a monastery with a school attached to it, and a number of families came out to farm the land and raise children there. Senan had plenty of good company to cheer him in his age.

There was one last lucky thing in his life. He was told the exact moment when he would die, so he was able to plan his work to the last hour and see it finished and tidy with no odd ends left to worry the man who would take charge after him.

And that is a blessed thing in anyone's life.

Werburgh and the Troublesome Geese

St. Werburgh was born a princess. Her paternal grandfather was old King Penda of Mercia, he who slew five kings of whom two were saints. He was a pagan, stubborn and unchanging as the hills until the day he died, but his son Wulfere, who was Werburgh's father, turned Christian and founded an abbey where saintly men might live together away from the world.

Descended on both sides from warrior-kings, the girl might herself have married a king and raised sons of her own to be fighting-men, but that was not the life she chose. When her father, Wulfere, died, she covered her bright hair with a nun's veil and entered the convent of Ely to be a bride of Christ. Thus, instead of managing a great household with stewards and servants to wait upon her lordly guests, she occupied herself with the small domestic matters of a house of women and, with her own hands, served the poor. She was devout and gentle and patient, but shrewd and capable too, like all her kin. Though generous to the humble and to those who had been unfortunate, she could strike a hard bargain with those others who could afford to pay, and no one cheated the pious ladies while Werburgh had control of the money-chest. She was known everywhere as a peace-maker, and settled disputes among nuns and townsfolk alike; it was said that even the starlings hushed their quarrelling when she came near—but that may not have been strictly true, for starlings are not reasonable birds.

The convent prospered and Werburgh's uncle, King Ethelred, thinking it shame to waste so much talent in one house, gave her the headship of all the monasteries for women which were in his realm of Mercia, and from that time she travelled from one to another, between Ely, Trentham, Hanbury and Weedon.

There are convents where the visitation of a superior throws all into uproar, where the household books are scanned by trembling nuns, fearful of having to explain this item or that, to apologize for such needless extravagances as wax candles instead of tallow, to make excuses for the shortage of eggs or the failure of the herb-garden, or the expense of a rebuilt wall. But it was never so where Werburgh came—for her even ducks laid where their eggs might be found without trouble, and the poor who had been helped through the lean winters gave their labour with goodwill. The most scatter-witted of cellaresses might submit her accounts to the visitor's scrutiny, secure in the knowledge that she had done her best and would be scolded neither for blots nor greasy thumb-marks so long as the balance at the end of each page agreed.

'She is firm but she is just,' the nuns told each other. 'And whatever is wrong, she will soon set right.' Nevertheless they worked hard to ensure that nothing would be wrong.

Yet there was something *very* wrong at one of her houses.

St. Werburgh arrived in the dusk of an evening and was made welcome. The Prioress herself led the way to the guest-room and poured cool, herb-scented water into a bowl that her superior might wash away the dust of travel from her hands and face. There were fresh rushes strewn on the floor, and the bed was clean and new-made. All was as it should be in a well-ordered house—and yet Werburgh sensed that something was not well. The Prioress was not entirely easy in her welcome and seemed to be listening, not to what her guest said, but for some other sound. And that not a pleasant one.

'What sound?' thought Werburgh, and she too listened. But there were only familiar country noises, the sudden hiss and gobble of geese disturbed by the distant yelp of a fox in the woods beyond the convent wall, and the raucous cawing of rooks wheeling home to the great elms behind the mill.

'Well, whatever the matter, it will be uncovered before long,' thought Werburgh, and she followed the Prioress to the refectory where the nuns gathered for their evening meal.

St. Werburgh looked at the two long rows of silent ladies and wondered at their pale faces and lack of animation. Perhaps they were keeping too strict a rule, too bloodless a diet. But no—not even her grandfather could have found fault with the fine roast goose the Cellaress was carving, nor with the stuffing of eggs and parsley, ginger, cinnamon, saffron and onions.

'You keep a good table,' she said to the Prioress, who merely bowed in response.

'At least we have geese,' said the Cellaress. And one of the younger novices shuddered.

St. Werburgh laid aside her knife.

'You are troubled by your geese?' she asked. And now everyone began to talk at once.

'They have destroyed the garden...'

'They trample the herbs with their great feet...'

'They bruise the tender leaves with their hard beaks...'

'They chase the lay-sisters from their work...'

'They disturb us at our prayers...'

'They snap at our heels when we kneel in devotion...'

'They invaded the orchard and held Sister Frideswide a prisoner in an apple tree for the whole afternoon, from nones to compline...'

'Our Fridays are without fish for they will not let our man, Hob, near the fish-pond...'

'We have geese,' said the Cellaress, 'though we have little else.'

'Tell me how this has come about,' said St. Werburgh to the Prioress.

'It is true,' said the Prioress, 'though I had meant to spare you our troubles until tomorrow—perhaps even to have hidden them from you during the whole of your stay with us, for there is nothing you can do. And after all,' she added, 'it is a small thing to be weighed against the suffering of the martyrs...'

'If the creatures hinder your devotion,' said St. Werburgh, 'it is enough. Come, with God's help I have settled disputes between men whose hands were on their knives; I have even settled disputes between nuns over questions of precedence, and God knows how thorny those matters can be. Eat now, and go to your prayers. I will speak to the geese tomorrow.'

The next morning, after prime, St. Werburgh went with the Prioress to the fowl-yard, but the geese had already wandered abroad. Some were in the herb-garden eating whatever they did not spoil, some were in the orchard guarding the trees, and one grey gander was in the mill-

stream, fouling the fishing-line that Hob had set. Shrieks from the direction of the cloister-garth told that the unruly birds had penetrated there and were harrying the ladies at their exercise.

'You see how it is,' said the Prioress. 'But I doubt that the Lord will want to be troubled over such a ridiculous plague as this.'

St. Werburgh went to the gate of the herb-garden and waited for the geese to come to her, which they did in their own slow time, scented with fennel, sage, tansy and marjoram as though ready for the carving-dish. They watched her with their bright, spiteful eyes, and threatened her ankles with their golden beaks, but St. Werburgh stood firm and shook her head at them.

'I am not angry with you,' she said, 'but sorrowful. . .'

They waited, listening.

'I have heard ill things of you,' she said, 'that you give my sisters no peace. You tear up the plants they have tended with such care, you keep them out of the orchard where they have every right to be, you deprive them of their fish. And even worse, you disturb the prayers that are our duty before all other things. Yet God has given the world to be ours as well as yours—there is enough for us all to share, and you are free of the sky too, as we are not. Why should you torment us so?'

The geese watched her and said nothing.

'Surely we are all part of God's creation,' said St. Werburgh. 'I can tell that you know it, for you walk proudly on the earth, and hold your beaks high as though you praise God with every step you take. But my sisters are humble and fear you. Can that be right?'

The geese conferred together, gobbling and stretching their long necks. Some scattered to every part of the convent acreage and returned, bringing others to hear what the saint had to say to them. The gander brought a fish in his beak and put it down, still flapping, at St. Werburgh's feet.

'Be off with you now,' she said. 'And think of my words. Surely we can live together without fuss.'

For the rest of that day, the nuns went about their work undisturbed. They tidied the garden and set snapped-off stems to grow in little pots; they gathered eggs in the fowl-yard and apples from the orchard; they walked in the cloisters and prayed in the chapel, and thanked God for St. Werburgh's way with geese. Hob fished in the stream and tickled for carp in the pond and that night there was fish on the table.

Yet the next day, all was as before. There were geese in the orchard and in the garden, in the cloisters and in the chapel, in the almonery and in the chapter-house. There were geese everywhere, except in the fowl-yard.

St. Werburgh went out with her eyes blazing. She was not King Penda's granddaughter for nothing and she was determined to have obedience from a flock of geese or know the reason why. But the great grey gander went to meet her and *he* scolded as much as St. Werburgh did. If she was angry, he was angry too and there was not a feather's difference between them.

While they faced each other there came a great noise of hissing and shouting from the end of the refectory building where the kitchen was, and a big white goose appeared in the doorway, dragging the cook—a stout, red-cheeked lay-sister—by a fold of her skirt, and two other geese chivvying her from behind, their wings outspread and their beaks darting at her calves.

'Lord ha'mercy!' cried the cook. 'Can no one protect

me from these devils of birds?' and she flailed about her with the skillet she held, but to no purpose at all. The geese were not afraid of her and merely jabbed at her legs the more ferociously.

The gander looked at the cook and hissed.

St. Werburgh looked at the cook and understood all.

'I think you have offended these good creatures,' she said, indicating the geese. 'Now, what can you have done to cause such commotion among them?'

'I?' demanded the cook. 'How may a poor, hard-working Christian woman offend a goose? I was in my kitchen, as is my place, and with no thought in my head beyond the blessed saints and the meal I was preparing for your good appetite. And what else should a cook be doing, but that?'

'Nevertheless, I think you are brought to justice,' said St. Werburgh. 'May I ask what you were preparing for my good appetite?'

'A pie,' said the cook. 'It's a miserable house that offers the same dish day after day. There was a roast goose for your welcome...'

'Your pardon,' said St. Werburgh to the geese.

'... and last night there was fish. And a grateful change we found it after all these weeks.'

'And tonight a pie,' said St. Werburgh. 'But what meat have you put beneath the crust, sister?'

'Why, a plump goose!' declared the cook, and screamed as all the geese in the garden made for her.

St. Werburgh bade them hush, and turned again to the cook.

'Surely you are a great fool,' she said. 'Aye, and worse than a fool. Can you expect these good creatures to bide still and quiet while you, at your pleasure, take one after another for your pot? I mourn with them—and I mourn for you too that you should be such an addle-pate. Go, sister, and fetch the pie.'

Two geese accompanied the woman to the kitchen and back again. St. Werburgh took the great pie-dish in her hands and the geese stood around in a circle, ruffling up their breast-feathers and spreading their wings, and hissing.

'I will pray,' said the saint. 'And you had best pray too,' she said to the cook.

So the two bowed their heads and offered the pie to the will of God, while all the geese raised their heads and seemed to be praying too, in their own fashion. Old Hob, coming up the long meadow, was bemused by the sight and went home to tell his goodwoman that surely he had seen everything now—two holy ladies and a flock of geese praying over a pie.

But prayer is a wonderful thing.

The pie-crust cracked across and across again; pastry-flakes scattered on the earth.

'The bird was jointed and braised...' said the cook.

'Pray,' said St. Werburgh.

The pie-dish moved in her hands. It was heavy, and growing heavier.

'... in good onion gravy...' said the cook.

'Pray,' said St. Werburgh.

And the bones in the dish moved together. And the feathers in the sack at the kitchen door fluttered and frisked in a sudden wind, and came dancing together in a cloud to hover above the dish. St. Werburgh was brought almost to her knees by the weight of it until at last she could hold it no longer.

As she placed the dish on the ground, a plump young

goose stepped down from it, looking a little bewildered—but no worse than that.

That evening, when the nuns had finished their supper of vegetable soup, St. Werburgh cautioned them never to eat goose again.

'I have made a truce between you and them,' she said. 'And they will not grudge you an egg or two. But if I should ever hear of another pie such as the one we might have eaten tonight, why, sisters, I will leave you to the mercies of your geese. But because I wish to be fair, I have told the geese that the cook may take any one of them she finds straying in her garden, for it would not be just to favour the birds above the nuns.'

And that is how matters stood for hundreds of years until King Harry closed all the convents and scattered the nuns across the breadth of England. Perhaps the geese flew away and perhaps King Harry or his bailiffs ate them, who knows?

St. Paul and St. Antony

When Antony was a young man, with the beard still downy on his chin, he founded a monastery in the desert and settled there with a few monks for company, safe from the distractions of the world.

Then, when he was a little older, he found even that company distracting, so he built himself a cell—a stone hut the shape of a bee-hive—a little distance from the monastery. And here, for a long time, he was completely happy.

But as the years passed he noticed that he was watching the distant walls of his old monastery more often than he should, and wondering how matters stood there. He found he was straining his eyes for a glimpse of the monks as they went to and fro in the garden they had made on the edge of the desert.

'This won't do,' said Antony to himself. And he blocked up the door that faced the monastery, and opened another on the opposite side so that he could see nothing but emptiness with a few rocks. Now, he thought, he would not be interrupted.

But he could still hear the monastery bell calling the hours—and then he would break off, even in the middle of a prayer, to listen. He would look at the sky in order to tell from the height of the sun what office was being said, and then his imagination went to work on it. He could see, in his mind, the monks bowing before the altar and he could hear, in his mind, the words they chanted. It seemed to Antony that even the service of God might be a distraction.

He would have to move further away.

And further again.

Time passed and Antony was an old man with nearly ninety years behind him, living on his own in a cave far out in the desert with nothing to distract him at all except maybe a buzzard in the sky, or a tiny lizard the colour of emeralds.

And now it was his thoughts that bothered him. He was a saintly man—there was no doubt about that. He thought of God day and night and prayed continually for the salvation of mankind. He had no care for his own comfort, whether he ate or slept, or was burned by the sun or frozen when the sun went down, and there was not a single worldly desire that gave him a moment's trouble. Surely he might claim to be the saintliest of all the saints in the desert—the most pious, the most devout. . .

But this was a terrible vanity. It was worse than priding oneself on being richer than anyone else, or better looking. And what worth had any of his achievements if he could count them as a miser counts his gold? Antony would banish the thoughts and stand in the noonday sun to bring himself to his senses.

But it was no use. At night the thoughts would return to plague him. No one else could have given up as much as he had, surely. . .

Thus it went on—day after day, night after night. The thoughts were more distracting than ever the monastery bell had been, and he could not so easily get away from them.

However, he had a strong will. He had not overcome every worldly desire he had ever had merely to be defeated in the end by his own mind. He arranged his wretched thoughts in order and looked at them one by one, and one by one he sent them packing—until there were only two left. And these were very stubborn.

He was absolutely sure that, whatever his faults, he led the holiest life that was possible to man and that, in order to do so, he had travelled further into the desert than any other man had travelled.

And these thoughts he could not overcome.

Still he struggled with them—and one night he heard a voice call his name.

'Antony.'

Now this was not a voice in his head, he was quite certain. And there was no one with him in his cell. Antony went down on his knees, trembling.

The voice said, 'Antony, there is a man more holy than you are. Seek him out.'

And a voice in Antony's head, that he knew was his own voice, asked, 'But who? Where?'

'His name is Paul.'

Antony cried aloud, 'But where may I find him?'

And the voice, now very small and far away, said, 'In the desert. Further out.'

This was a great wonder—that the holy Paul still lived. His reputation was immense, as wide as the desert, as deep as the sky, but he had not been seen for years upon years, and then only at a distance. Nomads and herdsmen and wandering monks, finding themselves within sight of his hermitage, would turn aside and take a different road. Such a solitude as Paul's commanded respect.

'He must be old now,' thought Antony, struggling to remember how old he himself was. 'It must have been when the Emperor Decius was in Rome and killing all the Christians in the cities, that Paul came into the desert. But that was long ago. . .'

He thought again. 'It was about the time that I, myself, was born. Dear God—if Paul yet lives he must have more than a hundred years behind him. . .'

That made the matter imperative. A man as old as Paul might die at any hour, there was no time to be wasted.

Antony started out at once. He would not even wait till morning, and he took nothing with him except his stout staff to lean on.

He had lived for too long in the wilderness to have any fear of it. He knew its strange beasts—horned vipers and spiders that wove traps with doors to them, and dogs that hunted in packs and chuckled and laughed at night as though they were not dogs at all but earth-bound spirits—as well as he had known his brother monks. He knew the desert's illusions too and he was not fooled by them.

'I will believe in water when I taste it on my tongue,' he said. 'And I will believe in trees when I lie down in their shade.'

He was making for a blue haze of mountains on the horizon, a haze that neither shifted nor changed, and he walked with a sort of staggering stride that grew stronger rather than weaker as the day grew.

It was a little after noon, when the sun was beginning its slow drop towards evening, that he met with a strange creature that was like no desert illusion he had ever seen, and like nothing he had ever dreamed, and like nothing he had ever encountered in the flesh. It had the head and torso of a man, with a noble face and a great hairy chest, and arms that were well shaped and muscular—and this trunk was set in the body of a horse, with four strong legs and neat shining hooves that clattered on the stones. Antony had long ago read about such creatures and he knew well enough that this was a centaur. He also knew that such creatures do not exist, but are the products of a pagan imagination. He would have passed it by but it stood full in his path and jabbered at him in a language he could not understand, and it would not leave him until he had made the sign of the cross.

'I will pray for you,' said Antony, 'whether you exist or not.'

Now he went more warily, for he saw that the desert was full of dangers he had not guessed. A little further on he met another creature, smaller than the first, having the head and body of a youth, but with golden eyes like a goat's and with horns springing from its brow. This one had legs like the hind legs of a goat and it pranced like a goat, and shook its goat-like tail.

'And what might you be?' asked Antony.

And the creature whispered in his ear, 'I am a satyr, such as men once worshipped in the dark woods. Come, worship me, Antony, and we will make the world young and lively again.'

'That cannot be,' said Antony. 'Your day is over. But if you like, I will pray for you, and perhaps you will sleep easier.' And he went on.

Next he saw a smiling man, dressed like a merchant, who crossed the path ahead of him and left a bar of shining gold where he could not avoid stumbling against it.

Antony laughed at that, to think the Devil was so simple he would try to tempt a holy hermit with gold. And while he was laughing he thought of all the things such a weight of gold might buy—a fine chalice for his old monastery, a jewelled and gilded cross to be carried in procession, warm woollen blankets and sustaining food for Paul, who was surely dying even at this minute. He stooped to pick up the gold—but the satyr came leaping over the stones on its quick goat-feet and kicked the golden bar away from Antony's hand, and the centaur came and trampled it into the earth. They both looked severely at Antony and pointed towards the mountains, which were now quite near. If he pressed on, he would reach the foothills by sunset.

So he pressed on, thinking of the part those pagan creatures had played in holding him back from touching the Devil's gold, and remembering, too, that each in its own way had first tried to tempt him. It was a great mystery.

'Perhaps they represent my passions,' Antony said to himself. 'Suppose that the centaur...' but he found he was too weary for argument and it seemed of small importance after all. Since both had helped him in the task that God had set him, then surely it followed that they, too, had been sent by God to direct him.

'I have learned precious little in my ninety years,' said Antony.

By this time he had reached the foothills and night was falling. The way was treacherous and there were little rivers of loose shale between the rocks, so that he kept falling and cutting his hands and feet. Moreover, there was scarcely any light, only a thin pale sliver of moon like the rind of a cheese. Paul's cave might be

anywhere—this side of the summit, or the other side—
and Antony was on the point of deciding to go no further
until the sun had risen again, when he saw the paw-
marks of some large beast leading straight up the
mountainside.

With the events of the afternoon so strong in his mind,
he took this as an omen and followed the tracks. Soon he
smelt hyena and was aware of a lean grey shape moving
ahead of him. He could hear the creature's panting
breath, and wondered if it heard his own—but it took no
account of him at all.

Straight to the top of the mountain it led him, and
then down a steep slope which was almost too much for
Antony. By the time he reached the bottom he was
bruised and shaken almost senseless—and there was the
hyena slinking away through a crevice in the hillside,
into a cave so narrow and so well hidden that Antony
would have passed it a dozen times without seeing it. He
knew at once that this was the cave of the holy Paul.

The cave was full of light, and there was the hermit
lying on a rough couch of branches, with the hyena's
head on his lap. Antony dared not enter without
permission so he took a small pebble and knocked with it
upon the wall of rock. And the wall moved, sliding
across the entrance, leaving only a crack sufficient for a
man to speak through.

Antony put his mouth to the crack and begged to be
admitted. He could taste salt tears on his tongue and he
feared that his words would be unintelligible through
the sobs he could not hold back.

He tried again.

'I am alone,' he said. 'And I have come a long way to
find you, because God commanded it. I have walked

through the heat of the whole day, and even the pagan creatures that have no existence in reality have helped me and showed me the way. You receive wild beasts—why will you not receive me?'

There was no answer.

'Whether you admit me or not,' said Antony, 'it is all one now. I am an old man and I will stay here at your door until I die.'

Then the wall moved again and he was able to go inside, into the light, and to kneel down at the side of Paul's couch, closer to this saintly man than anyone had been for nearly a hundred years. And they talked and prayed together until the unearthly light in the cave grew dim and was replaced by the ordinary rosy light of sunrise.

'We will breakfast now,' said Paul. And a raven came flying down from a thorn tree outside the cave, carrying in its beak a whole loaf of bread, warm and golden as though straight from the baker's oven.

'Why, here is a miracle!' said Paul.

Antony agreed. 'But Elijah also was fed by ravens,' he said.

'Ah, *that* is not what I meant,' said Paul. 'I have grown accustomed to this raven, which has fed me for more than sixty years—but mark this. Each day—and for more than sixty years—this gentle bird. . .'

The raven stepped sideways along the ground, fluttered its great untidy wings and emitted a fearful croak.

'. . . this gentle bird has brought me half a loaf. Today I have a visitor, one that I neither expected nor properly welcomed—and today the raven brings a *whole* loaf, a double portion. That is indeed a miracle.'

'God sent me,' said Antony. 'He would not expect you to feed me from your own lack.'

They blessed the bread and shared it, giving the crust to the hyena and scattering crumbs for the bird.

Paul said, 'You have come in a good hour, brother Antony. God sent you to hear my last confession and comfort me before I die. When that is done, you must bury this old body of mine in the earth beside my shelter. This task is something neither a hyena nor a raven can do, good friends though they be.'

Then Antony wept again, for this was the first human voice he had heard for many years; this was a man who might have been his friend and teacher, and he, Antony, had come too late for anything save the performance of a service he could not desire.

'Take me with you,' he said. 'I too am old. I will hear your confession, and you hear mine. Then we will die together.'

'It is not right that any dead Christian should lie above the ground, to be worn away by the wind and weather,' said Paul. 'Two Christians lying so would make a double wrong. No, Antony. This is the duty God has put on your back—you cannot abandon it. But there is something else you may do, if you will, something that I have a mind for.'

'I will do it,' said Antony, 'because you are my friend and my master.'

Paul paused a long time and the breath rattled in his thin chest. He was growing very weak now, and Antony had to stoop his ear to Paul's mouth in order to hear his words, and the terrible rattle punctuated each one of them.

'I have a mind to lie wrapped in the cloak that was

given you by the blessed Athanasius,' he said. 'Will you fetch it for me . . . from the monastery you built when you were young. . . ?'

And this he said, not because he cared about how his body might be shrouded once his spirit was gone away, but so that Antony might be spared the long sorrowing hours of waiting by his death-bed.

'Now hear my confession,' said Paul. 'And then make haste.'

The confession took some time to make. Paul found in himself so many sins of pride, of apathy, of ingratitude, wastefulness and sloth, that an entire day passed before Antony was free to make the journey. And then he sped as though the wind carried him.

He used his strong staff as though it were a vaulting-pole and leapt across the desert like a man pursued by demons. For half a day he thought he rode the centaur's back and his ears echoed to the thud of galloping hooves—but perhaps it was his heart drumming, for he knew that no centaur existed except between the pages of a book.

He passed the cave where he had last lived, and the stone bee-hive shelter where he had lived before then, and the one he had built when he first left the monastery—and there before him were the grey walls he remembered, and the herb-garden with a few old monks ambling up and down in the sun.

Only then did he wonder how Paul, who had been so long away from the world, had known about the cloak the blessed Athanasius had given him and, at the same time, he knew why he had been sent to fetch it.

The monks hurried to greet him, if their stumbling could be described as haste. They were all old men now, and their lives so stilled that a snail's slow progress up a wall could hold them breathless.

But Antony would not stop. He would neither eat nor rest nor wash the dust from his weary body. In one movement he took the cloak and turned back to the desert. The monks thought they heard his voice calling, 'I am already too late!' but they could not be sure. The desert had a way of making words seem other than they were.

'Perhaps he was not here at all,' they said, and shook their heads doubtfully.

Antony came to his old cave again and passed it. He thought he saw a host of angels and prophets and martyrs moving together in a white brightness, with Paul among them, his face shining. Yet when he looked again, there was nothing but the dust dancing.

He came to the foothills, and there was the centaur with many others of his kind, and satyrs, and winged horses, and young women who were like walking trees, and these all wept as he came to them. And as he passed on his way up the mountainside, they faded until he could see the shapes of the rocks through them, and there was nothing but the sound of their grief. And he knew that Paul was dead.

And it was so. The empty body knelt at the entrance to the cave with the hyena guarding it, as a dog will guard its master's possessions until told to leave them. When it saw Antony it whimpered and crept away, leaving a space and a loneliness behind it.

Antony wrapped the cloak about the body of his friend and thought, 'Now I must give him Christian burial.' Paul had told him where he wished to lie, and there Antony carried him. It was not easy, for he needed both hands for the carrying and one hand for his staff, and another to steady himself as he went. It was a duty that needed time, and thought, and care, but at last it was done. Here was the place that Paul had chosen, a shelf of flat ground behind the cave, a thorn tree patterning the earth with spiky lines of shade, and the mountain wall protecting it on three sides. On the fourth side, the land fell away in a series of broken terraces dotted with bushes.

'It is indeed a good place,' said Antony aloud. Then his heart gave a jerk in his chest, and he sat down, despair filling every part of him that was not already filled with shame.

He said, 'Oh, Paul. I have failed you.'

For he, an old man who was himself no more than a cage of bones, had raced death across the desert and back in order to fulfil a dying man's last desires—and he had remembered only half of it. To fetch the cloak for a shroud—that was one thing. To bury the body of a saint—that was another. First he must dig a hole in the ground—and this was something Antony had forgotten. Even a fool would have brought some sort of digging-tool, but Antony, with his reputation for wisdom, had brought only the cloak of Athanasius.

'God, let me die now,' he said. 'I am not worthy to be alive.'

And it seemed as though God heard him, for there came two great lions, bounding towards him across the scrubby plain and from terrace to terrace, their lean bodies tawny in the sun and their manes bristling.

'So I am to be devoured,' said Antony. 'Well, it is a Christian death.'

But the lions had not come to attack him. They went to him and lay down at his feet, rolling on their backs, with their paws curled and the claws sheathed in their soft pads. They fawned about him, tracing a pattern around and around his legs, screwing up their eyes and making a deep pleased rumbling noise in their throats.

Antony stroked their chins and blessed them because they were beautiful creatures and made him forget his misery.

That was why they had waited, to receive the blessing of a saint; now they would serve him in burying another. They scratched with their hard, sharp claws on the surface of the earth and loosened it. Then they dug patiently, kicking the soil behind them, until they had made a grave that was long enough and deep enough and wide enough to hold the body of Paul.

When it was ready they stood near with bowed heads and drooping tails while Antony lifted the body and laid it down in the grave. They stayed until he scattered the earth again and pressed it down—and when that was finished they went away, side by side, along the terraces.

Antony prayed at the graveside and slept and prayed again. He longed for a voice to tell him that he might take Paul's place and live out his years in this lonely hermitage. Even a voice in his own head would have been enough to persuade him, but there was no voice at all.

Once again he set his face towards the desert, but this time there was no urgency. If the journey took a thousand years, it would not matter. The desert was empty. There was no centaur to point the way, no satyr to crave his worship, no Devil to tempt him with desires for gold or holiness.

His old cave seemed a haunted place. The little spring was dry and sand settled in the hollow rock where the water had bubbled. Even that did not matter—he would not live there again.

But at the monastery they welcomed him as though he had never been away, as though they—and he—had dreamed the intervening years. The bell called him in.

St. Wulfric, the Boy and the Bread

There was a time, in the old days, when St. Wulfric lived in a hermit's cell near Hazlebury Plucknett down in Somerset. He had chosen the place because it was quiet and beautiful, with no bustle to draw a man's mind away from the contemplation of his Maker. And the people were proud of having a holy man come to live among them. They would take him little gifts of food—a few apples or a cabbage or an egg or two—and sit with him for a while in the peace of the evening, not saying a word for fear of disturbing his thoughts. But there were other times when they needed advice or to have their children blessed, and then they were not backward in asking. And neither was the saint backward in giving.

This is the story of how he helped a poor widow-woman who lived nearby.

She had a hard life of it, this widow, and a whole string of little children to feed and look after. Of course they did as much as they could to help her—the youngest gathered sticks for the fire and the older ones worked from time to time on the farms nearby, scaring the crows or stacking hay, according to the season. Between a bit here and a bit there they managed to stay alive, but hardly more than that. In fact, they were all as thin and brittle-looking as dry twigs—that is, all except Dicky, and he was as fat as a young porker.

One day, when everything looked more than usually

bleak, the poor widow, with three of her smallest children, climbed the hill to St. Wulfric's cell, not that she expected the good man to do anything for her but because she felt the need to unburden her heart of its trouble and St. Wulfric was known to have a sympathetic ear.

'Mustn't go empty-handed,' she said. 'I may be poor but I know what's what.' And she had taken the last thin little flat oatcake from the bread-crock and wrapped it in a clean, white rag.

But when the three little children saw her give the precious oatcake to St. Wulfric, they burst into tears. They could not help themselves.

St. Wulfric saw how it was with them. He looked into their sad, pinched little faces and said, 'There now, don't cry. Go down to the spring just round the bend of the hill, and see what the birds have left for me today. Take this basket and bring back whatever you find on the flat stone near where the water bubbles up.'

So they dried their eyes and off they went, with the smallest one in the middle. He was so tiny that a lamb could have knocked him over, but he was determined to go. And back they came with the basket so full they could only push it—their thin little arms weren't strong enough to lift it from the ground.

'Well, now,' said St. Wulfric. 'My birds must have known you were coming. Here's bread and fresh butter and a crock of cream. So I'll just put your mother's good oatcake up here on the shelf for the moment.'

Then they all sat down in the sunshine to eat, and those children had never tasted such a meal in their lives. When they had finished every last crumb the saint sent them off to play on the hill and then he turned to the widow.

'Now,' he said. 'You didn't toil all the way up from the village just to show me your little ones, I'll be bound. You've trouble on your heart and need to unload a bit of it, so come, I'm ready and listening.'

'It's our Dicky,' said the widow. 'He's a good enough boy in his way and he works hard, but he's thoughtless.'

St. Wulfric nodded his wise old head. 'And he's eating you out of house and home,' he guessed.

'I'm not speaking against the boy,' said the widow anxiously. 'Don't think that. He's my own and I love him dearly, but life is hard and I don't know whatever I shall do.'

'Of course you don't,' said the saint. 'Love is a grand thing—but it can get in the way of clear-thinking sometimes. Tell me all about it.'

'It's his appetite,' said the widow. 'It seems he can never get enough to eat. . .'

And no more do the others, thought St. Wulfric, but he let the widow tell her story to the end.

'He gets plenty at Farmer Mellish's,' she said. 'Our Dicky's the bird-boy at Mellish Farm; they're great eaters down there and they don't stint him. But all the same, when he comes home at night he gollops up everything he can find in the house, and he don't think to ask if the others've had theirs. If his brothers are in work, *they* bring home vittles to share, scraps of meat and maybe a turnip or a bag of greens, but if our Dicky be about he grabs that too. Often the little ones cry themselves to sleep from hunger. . .'

Thinking of that made the poor soul weep a little herself, and it was a while before she could continue. The saint sat quietly and looked at the oatcake on his shelf and thought what he would do.

'Then he gets up in the night,' said the widow. 'And he hunts about, and if there's anything I've saved for breakfast, he has that as well, and the others go to work empty. It's all very well for him—he gets his dew-bit, his morning snack, at Mellish's. But I dursn't be hard on him, master, he works hard and needs filling, his father was the same—only things were easier, those days.'

'Tell him I would like to see him,' said St. Wulfric. 'There's no harm in my having a word with the boy.'

Then he told the widow to go home and take the children with her, and he blessed them all before they went.

'They won't be hungry tonight,' he said. 'And who can tell what tomorrow will bring?'

So early the next evening Dicky came up the hill to St. Wulfric's cell. He was a *very* fat boy and breathless from the climb, though the hill was certainly not a steep one. He was surly-tempered too, and resented having to turn out again as soon as he had got home, all because an old fool with a long white beard had expressed the wish to see him.

'Well, what do you want?' he said to Wulfric without a word of greeting.

'Only that you should take some food to your mother,' said the saint. 'It's on the shelf there. Take any bread that you see, and give it to her with my blessing. But be as quiet as you can for it is time I was at my prayers.'

He turned his back on the boy, and knelt down on the stone floor with a great creaking of his old knees.

Dicky looked on the shelf and at once caught sight of his mother's oatcake, crisp and golden on the white cloth. So that's where it was! He knew there should have been one left in the crock and he'd searched for it a long

time the night before. And his mother had given it to this silly old man! He felt as outraged as though they had connived together to steal it from him.

There were two big white cottage loaves on the shelf beside the oatcake and Dicky took those too and then hurried away as fast as such a fat boy could, which indeed was not very fast at all.

Before he had gone far he was hot and exhausted and in need of a bite to keep his strength up, so he sat down on the grass with his great fat legs stretched out in front of him, and ate one of the loaves. It was delicious, even better than Mistress Mellish's baking, and she had a name in those parts for the lightness of her bread.

Having eaten the first of the loaves, Dicky thought he might as well eat the second—there was no sense in taking just one home to feed a family as large as his. And when he had eaten that, he looked again at the oatcake. If he took the oatcake home surely his mother would be hurt and offended, thinking the saint had rejected it. It would be a kindness to eat the oatcake.

He had not a morsel of guilt about it and set off home in quite a cheerful frame of mind to see if his younger brother, Timmy, had brought anything back for supper. But his sense of well-being lasted for only a little while. He began to have terrible pains inside as though he had eaten a dozen stones and hooks and knife-blades. By the time he reached his mother's cottage he was feeling so ill that he could not even cross the threshold. He could only sit on the doorstep and groan.

Out came his mother, smiling like a queen, and what did she do but hand him a huge crust of white bread all smothered with butter?

'There you are, Dicky,' she said. 'Here's a fine, big

slice for you, for being such a kind, good lad and fetching those three loaves from the saint. 'Tis lovely bread, this, just like we ate yesterday.'

Dicky had looked very pale indeed when he sat down on the doorstep but now, when his mother said that, he turned even paler.

'What three loaves?' he stammered, and his stomach gave a sort of lurch.

'Why, the oatcake, and the two big cottage loaves all ready and buttered,' she said. 'I found them on the table, exactly where you must have put them. So you eat up, and you shall have another slice. I know that you're always hungry and tonight there's plenty for all of us.'

Then Dicky felt very frightened. He knew he had eaten all the bread from the saint's shelf and that it had no business at all to be there, sliced and buttered, on his mother's table. His stomach was hurting and he felt full to the top of his head—but his hand kept carrying the crust to his mouth, and his teeth kept biting pieces from it and chewing them up, and his throat kept swallowing. And it seemed to have nothing to do with him in the least.

'I'll have to go back to the saint,' he cried. 'There's something I forgot to say. You can give the other slice to Timmy...'

And he began to run—really to run—as he had never run before.

'I'll keep it for you,' his mother called after him.

When Dicky reached the hermitage on the hill, St. Wulfric was still on his knees with his back to the door. And there, on the shelf above his head, were the two white loaves and the oatcake, seeming to dance a gleeful little jig in the candle-light. Dicky just stood there in the doorway and shook with fear.

The saint finished his prayers and stood up.

'What, back again, Dicky?' he said. 'You must be hungry after so much walking. Will you have a piece of bread and butter now?' He reached up his hand for a loaf.

Dicky started to cry, but he dared not refuse. It took him an hour to eat that slice, and the taste of it stayed on his tongue for days, but afterwards he was a different boy entirely. He never again took more than his share of whatever food was in the house, and every single day he saved some of his dinner and brought it home for the little ones.

'He'll fade away,' said Mistress Mellish in alarm. But it didn't come to that. Indeed, he grew to be a fine, generous young man and took care of his mother until the end of her life. And as he grew older he spent quite a few of his evenings sitting peacefully in St. Wulfric's cell, smoking his pipe and watching the sun set over the edge of the world.

One evening he said, 'But why the oatcake? The bread was your own and there was something strange about it—but what had the oatcake to do with it all?'

'It was to show the bread where it had to go, of course,' said the saint. 'Otherwise it might have gone anywhere.'

Even then Dicky could not quite fathom it out. Can you?

SOURCES

In writing these stories I am especially indebted to Butler's *Lives of the Saints*, four thick volumes; Sigrid Undset's *Sagas of the Saints*; Lady Gregory's *Saints and Wonders*; Andrew Lang's *Book of Saints and Heroes* and *Saints and their Beasts* by Helen Waddell. The stories of St. Werburgh and St. Wulfric and St. Christopher I heard as a child and have never forgotten them.

It may interest readers to know that ancient writers refer to a commentary on Obadiah that St. Jerome was known to be writing, but it has never been found. I like to think that it may have been lost because of the rumpus with the lion.

Ursula Synge

DATE